ASK ME TOMORROW

CW00548343

A Pla

by

STAN BARSTOW and ALFRED BRADLEY

based on the novel by

STAN BARSTOW

SAMUEL FRENCH

LONDON

NEW YORK   TORONTO   SYDNEY   HOLLYWOOD

FOR AMATEUR PRODUCTION ENQUIRIES

UNITED   KINGDOM   AND   WORLD
EXCLUDING NORTH AMERICA
plays@samuelfrench.co.uk
020 7255 4302/01

Each title is subject to availability from Samuel French,
depending upon country of performance.

ASK ME TOMORROW

Produced by Sheffield Repertory Company Ltd at the Playhouse
Theatre, Sheffield, on the 18th February 1964 with the following
cast of characters:

(in the order of their appearance)

WILF COTTON	*David Neal*
MARGUERITE FISHER	*Angela Thorne*
MRS POPPY SWALLOW	*Elspeth Macnaughton*
SYLVIA	*Anne Stallybrass*
HARRY COTTON, Wilf's brother	*Roger Rowland*
A MAN	*Brian Huby*
RONNIE BETLEY	*Michael Warchus*

Directed by GEOFFREY OST

SYNOPSIS OF SCENES

*The action of the play passes in Mrs Poppy Swallow's house in a
fairly large industrial city in the West Riding of Yorkshire*

ACT I

SCENE 1   A midsummer afternoon
SCENE 2   Evening, several days later
SCENE 3   Evening, a week later

ACT II

SCENE 1   Evening, a week later
SCENE 2   Later the same evening

ACT III

SCENE 1   The following evening
SCENE 2   An autumn night, ten weeks later
SCENE 3   Late afternoon, two weeks later

Time—the present

*It is suggested that the play may also be performed in two Acts,
with one interval only, i.e. between Scenes 1 and 2 of Act II.*

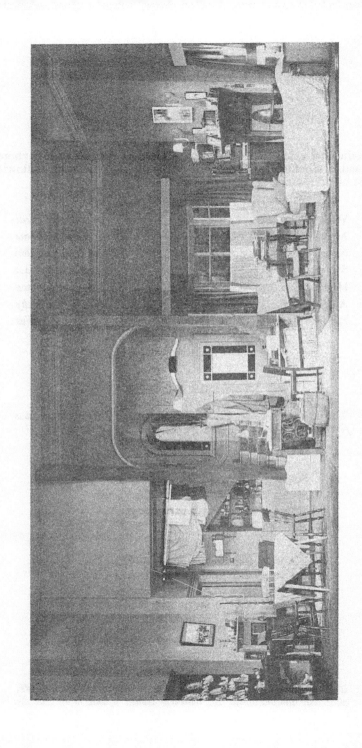

ACT I

SCENE I

SCENE—*Mrs Poppy Swallow's house in a fairly large industrial city in the West Riding of Yorkshire. A midsummer afternoon.*

The house stands in a district of well-built Victorian villas, well-to-do before the motor car began to take the industrialists and executives out beyond the city boundaries. It is a composite setting, showing most of the ground floor of the house, with the entrance hall C, *the kitchen* R *and Wilf's bed-sitting-room* L. *Wilf's room is what was once the drawing-room with a bay window up* C *overlooking the front garden and street. The fireplace is* L *and a door* R *gives on to the hall. There is a small window down* L. *A door at the back of the hall opens on to an inside lobby or porch with the front door* L. *The stairs,* R *of the hall, lead up and off* R. *The door to the kitchen is at the foot of the stairs,* R *of the hall. In the kitchen, there is a door up* R *leading to the scullery and a fireplace with an old-fashioned oven in it is* R. *Wilf's room is simply furnished, and rather shabby, but with little of the "Stag at Bay" or "aspidistra" atmosphere about it. There is a gas fire installed in the boarded-up fireplace aperture. There is a divan bed down* L, *with a cover over it. A rather splendid, though well-worn wing armchair, upholstered in wine-coloured velvet, stands* L, *beside the fire. A second armchair is* C. *Against the wall* R *is Wilf's work-table on which there is a portable typewriter, usually surrounded ·by a litter of folders, notebooks and pages of typescript. There is an upright chair at the table* R, *and a pouffe below it. Between the table and the door is a set of low bookshelves, stuffed rather haphazardly with books and magazines. An occasional table stands in the window bay, with an upright chair* L *of it. In the alcove above the fireplace is a chest of drawers, with some painted shelves on the wall over it. A small cabinet stands down* L. *At night, the room is lit by wall-brackets over the fireplace, a table-lamp on the cabinet down* L, *and a desk lamp on the table* R. *The switch is below the door* R. *In the hall there are hooks for coats* R *of the porch door, over which hangs a set of bull's horns. In the angle of the staircase, there is a large Chinese vase filled with bulrushes. At night the hall is lit by a shaded pendant* C, *with the switch* L *of the porch door. The kitchen is furnished as a living-kitchen. The furniture is nondescript: a table* C, *with three chairs,* R, L *and above it, an armchair above the fireplace and a sideboard against the wall down* R. *There is a cupboard with shelves over it, up* C; *and a television receiver stands below the fireplace. A creel hangs under the ceiling up* C, *usually with freshly ironed clothes hanging from its bars. At night the room is lit by a shaded pendant* C, *with the switch above the door up* R.

When the CURTAIN *rises, it is a grey, rainy day. After a moment,* WILF COTTON *enters from the scullery up* R *in the kitchen, carrying a glass of milk. He crosses the kitchen and hall and goes into his room. He is a lean, dark, wiry young man of twenty-two or three. He usually wears a sweater and slacks. Though not unkempt, he is apt to be careless about his appearance. He is a mixture of moods, sometimes modest, sometimes apparently conceited and slightly sententious, though on occasions when he moralizes or pontificates he deliberately adopts a pompous manner to cover his real feelings with humour. He is, under all this, capable of great tenderness and warmth of feeling. Though there is no mistaking his working-class origins, his accent is not too obtrusive. He picks up some sheets from the table R and drinks the milk as he looks at them. The front-door bell rings. WILF puts down the glass, goes into the hall and opens the front door.*

WILF. Oh, good afternoon.

MARGUERITE (*off*) Is Mrs Swallow at home? I believe she's got a vacant room.

WILF. Oh, the room. Will you come in?

(MARGUERITE FISHER *enters by the front door. She is an attractive girl, a little younger than Wilf. She has an air of good breeding and can be chillingly cool if anyone offends her. This is in many ways a defence against the world, which has treated her badly on several occasions. Just now, although interested in her surroundings, she gives the feeling that she is holding herself in on a tight rein. She carries a suitcase and her handbag*)

Actually, Mrs Swallow's out, but she won't be long. (*He motions to the door of his room*) You can wait in here if you like.

MARGUERITE. Thank you. (*She goes into Wilf's room and puts her case on the floor just inside the door*)

(WILF *follows Marguerite into the room*)

WILF (*crossing to the fireplace*) She's just popped up the road to the shops. She shouldn't be more than a few minutes. This is my room, actually. (*He indicates the armchair* C) Sit down.

MARGUERITE (*moving* C) I hope I'm not disturbing you. (*She motions to the typewriter*)

WILF. Oh, no, that's all right. I'm glad of an excuse to break off really. I feel a bit guilty about it. I've just had a bout of flu and if I can do this I could be doing my work at the office. But the doctor says I mustn't go back this week so I suppose that salves my conscience a bit.

MARGUERITE (*sitting in the armchair* C) I don't think it pays to go back too quickly; but you'd be better off outside, getting some fresh air.

WILF. That's what Poppy says—Mrs Swallow. But it's not too warm out and I might catch a chill. Then where would I be? (*He smiles at her*)

(*There is a small awkward pause*)

Er, I'm afraid I don't smoke, so I can't offer you a cigarette.

MARGUERITE. I've got some here. (*She takes a cigarette from her handbag*)

(WILF *takes a box of matches from the mantelpiece and lights Marguerite's cigarette*)

WILF (*sniffing luxuriously at the smoke*) That smells marvellous.
MARGUERITE. Do have one. I thought you said you didn't.
WILF (*a little ruefully*) I don't—as of ten days ago. But you carry on. It'll do my will-power good.

(MRS POPPY SWALLOW *enters by the front door. She is a handsome, well-built woman in her early forties. She dresses simply, with no startling sense of fashion, but this does not detract from her chief charm which is an essential womanliness. She combines warmth and sensuality in a way that makes men see her as mother or older sister as well as possibly a lover. She sometimes exaggerates her North-country accent for effect. She carries a shopping bag*)

That'll be Poppy now. Excuse me a minute. (*He goes into the hall*) Oh, Poppy, there's somebody arrived to join the madhouse.
POPPY. Madhouse! Well, it was all right before you came. (*She puts her bag on the floor in the hall and goes into Wilf's room*)

(WILF *follows Poppy into the room*)

(*To Marguerite*) Good afternoon. Come about the room, have you?

(MARGUERITE *rises under* POPPY's *appraisal*)

MARGUERITE. Yes, the woman at twenty-two—Mrs Randall—told me about it. I went there first but her room was taken.
POPPY. Have you come far, Miss—er . . . ?
MARGUERITE. Fisher. Marguerite Fisher. From London. I arrived yesterday.
POPPY. All that way. Come up to a new job, have you?
MARGUERITE. Well, not exactly. I intend to look for a job. Something secretarial. I shouldn't have any trouble after the kind of work I was doing in London.
POPPY. I see. Well, I expect you intend stopping a while, now you're here.
MARGUERITE (*a little coolly*) That will depend mainly on whether I like living here. If I might see the room . . .

(POPPY *looks Marguerite up and down*)

POPPY. Aye, the room. Well, happen you're lucky Mrs Randall was full up. I flatter meself this room's a cut above owt she's got to offer.
MARGUERITE. Oh, I shouldn't have taken it. One look through the front door was enough for me.
POPPY (*chuckling*) Aye, it would be. Reason I ask if you're likely to be stopping is because I like my people to give me time to get to know 'em. You can get some rum characters on your doorstep. I never have catered for a floating population and I don't intend to start. I like to get on well with my people and them to get on with

me. Like Wilf here. Just look at him. I've been trying to fatten him up since the day he walked into the house and it hasn't made a ha'porth of difference. He doesn't get enough fresh air and exercise. All day in a stuffy office and then cooped up with that typing machine at night.

WILF. Knock it off, Poppy.

POPPY. I'm telling you. I'll bet you haven't put your nose outside this house today. Anyway, you get on with it while I show this young lady upstairs. (*She goes into the hall*)

(MARGUERITE *follows* POPPY *into the hall*)

I think you'll find it's a very pleasant room. The back of the house gets all the sun first thing. The furniture that's in you can shift about as you like so long you don't do any damage.

(POPPY *and* MARGUERITE *exit up the stairs.* WILF *moves to the table* R *and picks up his papers.*
      SYLVIA *enters by the front door. She is a rather seedy blonde of indeterminate age. She goes to the foot of the stairs but hearing somebody up there she taps on* WILF's *door*)

WILF (*turning*) Who is it?

(SYLVIA *opens the door and looks in*)

Oh, hello, Sylvia.

SYLVIA. Who's Poppy got with her, Wilf?

WILF. A girl wanting a room.

(SYLVIA *comes into the room*)

What are you doing home at this time? It isn't half-day closing.

SYLVIA (*pulling a face*) Two guesses.

WILF. I thought you were all settled down there.

SYLVIA. Aye, so did I. An' I was till Mr Frobisher's wife came an' found us in the back room the other day. We weren't up to anything, either, so you can take that look off your face. Trade was slack so we were just sitting having a chat. It's the only place to sit down. Anyway, his missis walked into the shop an' found us.

WILF. She didn't accuse you of anything, did she?

SYLVIA. No, she just looked. But I got the message. She got to work on him after, and this morning he went all round the houses telling me it wasn't his wish and he'd always found me satisfactory, but he'd really have to let me go.

WILF. But didn't he give you any notice?

SYLVIA. Aye, he did. And I told him where to put it an' walked out. Him! Five foot nowt, bald, glasses and a hearing aid. As if I'd get up to owt with him. She must think I've got no choice. (*She wanders disconsolately* L) It's a shame, though. I was just catching up with me rent arrears and that silly jealous old bitch has to stick her nose in. I don't know what I'll say to Poppy.

WILF. Oh, it'll be all right, Sylvia. I'll back you up if it comes to it.
SYLVIA. Will you, Wilf?
WILF. 'Course I will. After all, it wasn't your fault, was it?
SYLVIA. Oh, no, I couldn't help it.

(WILF *turns aside with a little smile, knowing that possibly* SYLVIA *is not as innocent as she makes out*)

WILF. Well, that's okay, then.
SYLVIA. Aye. Thanks ever so much, anyway, Wilf. (*She crosses to the door and looks discreetly out*) I'll nip up and make meself scarce while Poppy's busy. You won't say anything till I've seen her, will you?
WILF. Cub's honour.
SYLVIA. You'd look all right in shorts, too.

(SYLVIA, *with a little giggle, goes into the hall and exits up the stairs. WILF sits at the typewriter and studies his papers*)

WILF. Ugh! A fine day's work this is. (*Suddenly he takes some sheets in his hand and rises with one thumb holding the sleeve of his sweater as though tucked into the armhole of a waistcoat. In a deliberately broadened West Riding accent he begins to deliver a pompous address to an imaginary gathering*) "Gentlemen of the Academy. It is a signal honour you do me here today in awarding me the Nobel Prize for Literature. In a long and not undistinguished career I place this second only to the gold medal presented to me at the Cleckheaton Triennial Festival of Dialect Poetry and Handbell-ringing for my little folk poem entitled *Grit*. If I might refresh your memories, gentlemen, by quoting just a few lines."

(MARGUERITE *enters down the stairs*)

> "Put thi hand in mine, lad
> And dry that little tear.
> Thi mother's on the streets, lad,
> Thi father's on the beer."

(MARGUERITE *taps on* WILF'*s door*)

(*He calls*) Er—come in.

(MARGUERITE *comes into the room*)

MARGUERITE. I thought I heard voices.
WILF. I was thinking aloud.
MARGUERITE. I came down to get my case.
WILF. Oh, are you taking the room?
MARGUERITE. Yes, it looks very nice.
WILF. Well, I'm glad you're staying.
MARGUERITE. Thank you. Have you lived here long?
WILF. About six months.

MARGUERITE. Is it your home town?
WILF. No, but I haven't come as far as you.
MARGUERITE. As it happens, I was born here.
WILF. You'll know it better than I do, then.
MARGUERITE. Oh, I doubt that. I moved away when I was quite small and I haven't been back since. There seem to be so many changes.
WILF. Yes, there's a lot of rebuilding going on. Some of it's pretty horrible, too. Still, the City Fathers say we must keep up with the times. Isn't it rather unusual, though, to come back here after living in London? It's usually the other way round.
MARGUERITE (*not to be drawn*) Oh, different people have different reasons. What are you doing, if it isn't frightfully secret? Are you writing a play?
WILF. No, a novel, actually.
MARGUERITE. Oh, should I have heard of you?
WILF. It's unlikely. My name's "Wilf Cotton".
MARGUERITE. No, I'm afraid I haven't.
WILF. You will one day, with a bit of luck.
MARGUERITE. And then I'll be able to say I once lived in the same house as the celebrated Wilf Cotton.
WILF (*smiling*) Yes, something like that.
MARGUERITE. Is it your first novel?
WILF. Well, to all intents and purposes, yes.
MARGUERITE. So I really can be excused for not having heard of you?
WILF. Oh, Lord, yes. Don't let that bother you. I've had a few short stories broadcast and there was a piece of mine in the last number of *Etude*—(*he crosses to the bookshelves on the wall up* L *and rummages in them*) but you don't make a name on that sort of thing.
MARGUERITE. *Etude.* I don't think I've heard of that.
WILF (*taking the magazine from the shelf*) One of those little magazines. (*He opens it and finds the place*) Run on a shoe-string. Half a dozen issues and they die the death. (*He moves to* L *of Marguerite and hands her the magazine*) They offer you a fiver for a contribution and then go out of business and send you a paperback copy of *Little Women* as a consolation prize. Not that it's happened to this one yet, but it's only a matter of time.

(MARGUERITE *looks at the magazine*)

MARGUERITE. A miner's son, are you? Another budding D. H. Lawrence?
WILF. I think the resemblances are superficial. (*He moves to the fireplace*) Have you read much of him?
MARGUERITE. A little. I started with the abridged edition of *Lady Chatterley* when it was passed surreptitiously round school as hot stuff. Then I read the Penguin when it came out.
WILF. Lots of people have heard of Lawrence who didn't know he existed before Penguin published *Lady Chatterley*.

(WILF *does not mean to be wounding but* MARGUERITE *is nettled by what seems to be his presumption. She returns the magazine to him and rather coolly changes the conversation*)

MARGUERITE. Really? How many other people live in the house?

WILF (*returning the magazine to the shelf*) Well, just at the moment there's only me and a woman called "Sylvia". She's a bit of a character.

MARGUERITE. Mrs Swallow's a widow, isn't she?

WILF. Yes, she is.

MARGUERITE. Why did the last person leave?

WILF. He's gone to Birmingham to join some relatives. He was a West Indian called "Appleyard Dearborn". He worked on the Corporation buses and studied engineering in his spare time. Didn't Poppy say anything about him?

MARGUERITE. No, she didn't.

WILF. Probably never thought to mention it. Anyway, she's changed the sheets since then.

MARGUERITE. I think we can take it, Mr Cotton, that my views on the colour question are as enlightened as yours.

WILF. Sorry. Only Poppy wasn't too popular with some of the neighbours for taking Appleyard in. They said it lowered the tone of the neighbourhood, though God knows it must have lost whatever tone it had round about the first world war. I'll give you a hand up with your case, if you like.

MARGUERITE. Don't bother, thanks.

WILF. It looks rather heavy.

MARGUERITE. I can manage it.

WILF (*shrugging*) Okay. (*He crosses and opens the door*) By the way, if you want any other bits of furniture or knick-knacks for your room, there's a good saleroom in town. I got this wing chair there for fifty bob.

MARGUERITE (*picking up her case*) Thank you. I'll remember.

WILF. I'll see you later, then.

(POPPY *enters down the stairs*)

MARGUERITE. Yes, I expect so. (*She goes into the hall*)

POPPY. I hope you'll be comfortable.

(WILF *pulls a face as Marguerite goes into the hall, realizing he has not got off to a very good start, but wondering why Marguerite should be so touchy*)

MARGUERITE (*going up the stairs*) Thank you. I'm sure I shall.

(MARGUERITE *exits up the stairs*)

POPPY (*calling after her*) I'll be making a cup of tea in a minute. (*She goes into Wilf's room*) What do you make of that one, then, Wilf?

WILF (*lightly*) Quite a bright, intelligent young woman. An nteresting addition to the household, I'd say.

POPPY. Interesting. Yes, that's what I was thinking. She looked a bit tearful just now, I thought.

WILF Tearful?

POPPY. You haven't upset her, have you?

WILF (*crossing to the fireplace*) Me? Oh, now, Poppy . . .

POPPY (*moving down* L *of the armchair* C) I nearly said something, and then I thought I'd best mind me own business.

WILF. You did right. She'll confide in you if she wants to. Anyway, she's probably tearful about the same thing that made her come up here from London without a job.

POPPY. I wonder what that is.

WILF. She'll tell us in time, if she wants us to know. Let's not get nosey.

POPPY. Who's nosey?

WILF. You are, Poppy love. A proper old Nosey Parker.

POPPY. Oh, am I?

WILF. With only the best motives, of course.

POPPY. She's only a bit of a lass.

WILF. She must be nearly as old as I am.

POPPY. Well, you're only a bit of a lad.

WILF. But interesting, for all that, eh?

POPPY. And conceited with it.

WILF (*moving to her*) Give us a kiss, Poppy love.

(POPPY *does not resist when* WILF *kisses her, but when he puts his arms around her and tries to prolong the embrace she pushes him away*)

POPPY. That's enough. There's a time and place for everything and I've got me work to do.

(WILF *looks quizzically at* POPPY. *The door bell rings*)

Now who can that be? This house is like a shop today. (*She goes into the hall and opens the front door*)

HARRY (*off*) I was looking for Wilf Cotton. I'm his brother.

POPPY. Oh, come in.

(HARRY COTTON *enters by the front door. He is three years older than Wilf and more sure of himself. There was a time in childhood when they were very close but they have grown away from each other over the years. There is a great deal in Wilf now that* HARRY *cannot fully understand and it brings out at times a somewhat condescending attitude towards him. He looks slightly comical in leather motor-cycling gear and a large coloured crash helmet*)

(*She indicates Wilf's room*) You'll find him in there.

(POPPY *picks up her shopping bag, goes into the kitchen and exits to the scullery.* HARRY *opens* Wilf's *door and goes into the room*)

HARRY. Now then, mate. So this is where you're hiding out, is it?

WILF (*surprised*) Well, well, if it isn't Harry. Come in, come in. Take your space suit off. What's up?

(HARRY *removes his helmet and unfastens his jacket*)

HARRY. Oh, nowt really. It's me mam. She was worrying and nattering because she hadn't heard a word in three or four weeks, so I said, "Look, if it'll set your mind at rest I'll run over on the bike after work one day and see what he's up to."

WILF. How did you know you'd find me at home at this time?

HARRY (*moving* C) I didn't. (*He puts his helmet on the armchair* C) I thought I might find out where your office was and pick you up after work. What are you doing at home, anyway?

WILF. I've had flu.

HARRY (*grunting*) I thought for a minute you might ha' chucked up your job because of your writing.

WILF. Not yet awhile, Harry. Not just yet.

HARRY. Do you like it better than the pit? (*He crosses to the fire and warms his hands*)

WILF (*shrugging*) Adding up wages for colliers or adding up wages for birds in a shirt factory, what's the difference?

HARRY (*blandly*) Better figures. Anyway, I can tell her you're all right, then?

WILF. You can. Perfectly all right.

HARRY. You change your underwear regular and brush your teeth night and morning.

WILF (*laughing*) And take a bath every Friday night.

HARRY. Well, you know how she is.

WILF. You can tell her I'm waited on hand and foot.

HARRY. Was that your landlady 'at let me in?

WILF. Yes, that's Poppy.

HARRY. A widow, isn't she? I wouldn't mind having her wait on me for a bit. Are you well in with her?

(WILF *recognizes the implications of Harry's question*)

WILF. Well enough. How is everything at home, then?

HARRY (*crossing to* R) Oh, just jogging along. Me mam natters as much as she allus did and the old feller's still as quiet as an old sheep. You want to come over and have a look, if you still know the way.

WILF. Aye, I shall have to come. I've been on my way for ages, but the weeks seem to slip by. You know how it is.

HARRY. Say the word and you can jump on the back of the bike now.

WILF. I've just had a bout of flu, mate. I don't want pneumonia. No, maybe I'll come at the weekend.

HARRY. She does worry, y'know.

WILF. I know, and I ought to write more often. (*He realizes that Harry will not understand but now that he has started he has to go on*) You see, even here it reaches out and tries to suffocate you—the village, home and all that. That's what I had to get away from. It's what I want to write about but if I hadn't got away from it I'd probably never have written anything else.

HARRY. You picked a dump of a town to run to. If you'd gone to London I could have understood it.

WILF. It's just far enough and just anonymous enough. I'm not ready for London yet. When I go there it'll be as a Somebody not a Nobody. They'll know about me because of what I've done.

HARRY. Your ideas are big enough.

WILF (turning on him) And you'll never understand them, Harry; not if you live till ninety. You're where you belong, a collier in a collier's world. I was the renegade, the one who had to be different. Now I'm between two worlds. I don't belong to either, but I'm more my own man than I've ever been and I'm doing what I have to do. I'm developing my talent, Harry. And I've got talent, make no mistake about that. I don't kid myself that I'm a world-beater— but somewhere, sometime people will talk about contemporary writers and they'll mention me. (He stops and then as if to prick the bubble of his own pride, adds with a wry grin) Even if it's only to say how bad I am. (He moves to the window and stares out for a moment)

(HARRY is silent for a moment, nonplussed by Wilf's outburst)

HARRY. I heard that last story of yours, on the wireless.

WILF. Oh?

HARRY. Aye, I was round at Ronnie Betley's. They had it on. He said to tell you how much he enjoyed it. He was saying he'd like you to call round when you're over. He's got one or two ideas you might be able to use. (He moves to the armchair L and sits)

WILF. I'm not going to peddle Ronnie Betley's propaganda for him. If he wants to preach the cause he can do it himself, not through me.

HARRY. Cause? What the hell are you talking about? There's only one cause for us, mate, and that's our rights. It's Ronnie's job to look after 'em. An' a damn sight better man at it than old Cuthbert ever was.

WILF. Cuthbert used to settle trouble. That's what a union secretary's for. Ronnie Betley makes it. That's the difference between them. (He sits in the armchair C)

HARRY. Oh, who the hell cares about him, anyway?

WILF. Well, you're his mate, aren't you? Or his wife's.

HARRY (startled) What do you mean by that?

WILF. I've seen you talking to her on the street, Harry. I hope you don't look at her like that when Ronnie's around.

HARRY. You see too much.

WILF. He's not a man to cross, Harry.

HARRY. No, and he's not the man to give June all she wants, either. I'm sure of it. Least, sometimes I'm sure of it. Most times I can't make up my mind whether she's starved and looking for a bit on the side or if she's just a cold-blooded teaser. One thing I do know: when she crosses her legs and shows her stocking tops, it's no accident.

WILF. In other words, she knows why you go down there.

HARRY. She must have a good idea.

WILF (*after a pause*) And she's playing up to you? Well, God knows I'm no judge, Harry, and women take a lot of fathoming. But don't you think you could be wrong? They always seem to be happy and it could be she'd be shocked if she knew what you were thinking about her.

HARRY (*after a pause; deliberately*) I know things about June that even Betley doesn't know.

WILF. Oh, how's that?

(*There is a long pause during which* HARRY *seems to be trying to decide whether to take* Wilf *into his confidence*)

HARRY. I'll show you summat. (*He rises, takes out his wallet and extracts a photograph which he looks at before handing it to Wilf*) Just have a look at that. What do you think of that, then?

(WILF *takes the photograph and whistles through his teeth as he looks at it*)

WILF. Where the heck did you get this?

HARRY. I've had it nearly a year. Remember me going to spend that weekend with Jackie Smithers in Sheffield? Well, we got in with a photographer in a boozer and he took us back to his place. He dabbled a bit in pin-up stuff and he fetched this big collection of pictures out for us to look at. I was flabbergasted when I saw June's photo there and I nearly blurted straight out 'at I knew her. But I kept me mouth shut an' afore we left I managed to slip the photo into me pocket.

WILF. It must have been taken some years ago.

HARRY. Oh, aye. Before she ever met Ronnie, I'd say.

WILF. Well, well, well! Very saucy. Very saucy indeed. (*He returns the photograph to Harry*)

HARRY (*looking at the photograph*) The teasing bitch.

WILF. D'you think Ronnie knows his wife used to pose for pin-up photos?

HARRY. I'm sure he doesn't. He thinks she's a lady.

WILF (*after a pause*) Well, if you ask me, Harry, I think June got what she wanted when she married Betley. All right, he might be a bit disappointing in some ways. She sees you fairly often, finds you attractive and can't resist giving you the come on. But you're nobody, Harry, and she's got Betley who might do anything. And if I know him he's not the type to stand for any messing about.

HARRY. You mean she might not mind having a roll with me, but is it worth the risk?

WILF. In a nutshell.

HARRY (*looking at the photograph*) Well, there's only one way to find out.

CURTAIN

SCENE 2

SCENE—*The same. Evening, several days later.*

When the CURTAIN *rises, the lights are on and the window curtains are closed.* MARGUERITE *is seated at Wilf's typewriter, typing.* WILF *is* LC, *reading pages of typescript.* MARGUERITE *finishes typing and pulls the sheet from the machine.*

MARGUERITE. There, that didn't take long, did it?

WILF (*crossing to Marguerite*) It really is very good of you, Marguerite. (*He takes the sheet from her*) I didn't mean to let you in for it when we were talking.

MARGUERITE. Well, it's true that I can do it so much quicker than you can. And anyway, it's practice for tomorrow.

WILF. This looks a real professional job now.

MARGUERITE. Do you mind!

WILF. What? Oh, sorry. You know what I mean. (*He crosses to the fireplace*)

MARGUERITE. Who will you send it to?

WILF. *Woman Today*, I think. I'm an old friend of the fiction editor.

MARGUERITE. Oh?

WILF. Yes, he rejects my stuff regularly, and times its return with sadistic glee so that it lands on the mat first thing Monday morning.

MARGUERITE (*turning her chair towards Wilf*) Why send your work to women's magazines?

WILF. There aren't many more markets for short stories in this country.

MARGUERITE. If they don't accept anything you can't be giving them what they want.

WILF. A conclusion I arrived at some time ago. The trouble is I don't seem to write what they want.

MARGUERITE. You'll have to learn to.

WILF. Look, I'm not a baker taking orders for a dozen buns of a certain size, shape and flavour. I'm a writer, with a personality. I write what I want to write and then look for a market for it.

MARGUERITE. It seems a hard way of going about it.

WILF (*moving towards her*) It's the only way for me. I've got to write the truth as I see it.

MARGUERITE. Anyway, I hope you're successful this time. I like the story very much. There's one thing I'm not sure about, though.

WILF. Oh, what's that?

MARGUERITE. You suggest she would be able to tell just by intuition that he was deceiving her.

WILF. You don't think it stands up?

MARGUERITE. It's just that it is possible for a woman to be deceived by the man she loves without suspecting anything at all.

WILF. You think so? (*He realizes that Marguerite is speaking from experience*)

(POPPY *enters the kitchen from the scullery and picks up two ironed shirts from the kitchen table*)

MARGUERITE. For quite a long time.

(POPPY *crosses, taps on the door of Wilf's room and enters. She is surprised to find Marguerite there and so much at home*)

POPPY. Oh, I didn't know you were here, Marguerite. I thought you might be needing these shirts, Wilf.

WILF. You sneaked in and took them while I was out, Poppy. I intended to send them to the laundry.

POPPY. You might have done eventually. When you hadn't a clean one to your back. Five I found. Rolled up in a ball under the bed. (*She crosses and puts the shirts on the bed*)

(MARGUERITE *smiles*)

WILF. Oh, well, thanks very much. You shouldn't have, though.

(MARGUERITE *rises and collects her handbag*)

MARGUERITE. It's time I was going up.

POPPY. Don't let me interrupt anything.

MARGUERITE. No, we've finished and I want an early start to-morrow. First day at the new job and all that. (*She picks up some manuscripts from the table* R) Do you mind if I take these other stories and read them?

WILF. If you like. I'll warn you, they're not all that good, though.

MARGUERITE (*moving to the door*) Now, now. No false modesty. Good night.

POPPY. Good night, love.

WILF. Good night, Marguerite, and thanks again.

(MARGUERITE *goes into the hall and exits up the stairs*)

POPPY. A nice lass, that.

WILF. Yes, she is. Very bright, too.

(POPPY *sits in the armchair* C)

(*He picks up the shirts and puts them in the chest of drawers up* L) Ah, Poppy, love, you're a great comfort to me.

POPPY. Am I?

B

WILF. You know you are. (*He sits on the arm of Poppy's chair and begins to snuggle his face into her neck, giving her little kisses*)

(POPPY *makes no response*)

POPPY. Let me know when you've finished.   .
WILF. I'm only just starting.
POPPY. I'd like to go to bed.
WILF (*smiling*) So would I.
POPPY. I'm not talking about that. (*She pushes Wilf from the arm of the chair*) I'm tired.
WILF. If you tell me you don't like it I won't believe you.
POPPY. I've told you, I'm tired.
WILF. What's the real reason, Poppy? An attack of the old Nonconformist guilt?
POPPY. Oh, you and your fancy talk. Save it for your books.
WILF. The chapel childhood, Poppy. It goes deeper than you think. Sex a monthly ritual in darkened rooms, with a suffocating weight of bedclothes and heavy breathing. I thought we'd agreed that it could be something superbly enjoyable between two grown people, with no strings attached. I thought you'd taught me that.
POPPY. I've taught you nothing. You knew all you needed to know when you came here. Two grown people, you say. Aye, one of 'em a lad with all his life in front of him and the other a woman with her best years gone. I'm old enough to be your mother, lad.
WILF. The world's full of women twenty years older than me who aren't my mother.
POPPY. How many of 'em do you go to bed with? How many of 'em teach you things?
WILF. Look, Poppy, we're two people. The twenty years are nothing—just an accident of birth.
POPPY. All right, then, if it's nothing why don't we make a right do of it and get married? Eh? That makes you think, doesn't it? You know that's plain damn silly, just like I do.
WILF (*moving and sitting on the desk chair*) I don't know what's come over you, Poppy. Does liking a person, being fond of somebody and wanting to make love, mean nothing else but marriage? That's surface morality, Poppy. I believe in warm honest relationships between people.
POPPY. That's a man talking, if ever I heard one. And a young one at that.
WILF. Oh, sure, bring the battle of the sexes into it and we'll never finish. What are we looking for, Poppy? Somebody to throw the blame on? Nobody's betrayed anybody. We both knew what was happening and what we were doing.
POPPY. It was my fault. I could have stopped it if I'd wanted to.
WILF. But you didn't want to, and I'm glad. I'll be eternally grateful that you didn't. (*He rises*) Don't you see what it's meant to me, all this? Don't you know?

POPPY. I could have stopped it before it started. That night you changed the bulb on the landing. Three or four months ago.

WILF. You're a handsome woman and I thought you were giving me an opening. And like most young men I don't look a gift horse in the mouth. Not an attractive gift horse like you.

POPPY. All laid on, was it? Only not a gift horse but an apple. A bit over-ripe but still good for plucking.

WILF. I can't defend myself, Poppy. There was nothing high-flown about my thoughts. Oh, I liked you as a person from the start but this was an unexpected development. I was flattered. I thought I was on to a good thing. She's dying for it, I thought, and it's all laid on for little me. I don't even have to go out in the rain to collect.

POPPY. I didn't know you could be such a nasty little devil.

WILF. I'm telling you this so I can tell you the rest. (*He kneels beside her*) You see, it wasn't the way you think. It wasn't that way at all. Afterwards, after that first time, I found that you meant a lot to me. You weren't just somebody I'd used and was done with till the next time. I'd always liked you and now I was fond of you. I wished I could do something for you. I wanted—I wanted to pluck happiness out of the air and give it to you in gratitude for what you'd given me. These times with you, Poppy, I think they've been the most wonderful thing that ever happened to me. Don't be sorry for them, love.

(POPPY *turns her head away.* WILF *realizes she is near to tears. He rises, moves behind Poppy's chair and puts his hand on her cheek*)

(*Gently*) What brought all this on, love?

POPPY. There's always strings. You can't get away from 'em. We're not just animals rutting in a ditch and there's always strings.

WILF. All strings have to be broken some time, Poppy. But don't say it hasn't been worth it, because it has.

POPPY. There's just summat not right about it, that's all.

WILF (*moving to the fireplace*) It's Marguerite, isn't it? You've been edgy with me ever since she came into the house.

POPPY. I look at her and I see myself, twenty years ago, full of hope and all my life before me; and I see you with her, the same generation. Seeing you together like that I feel like a mother watching her boy with his girl. And when you touch me it's like—like . . .

WILF. God, Poppy, you must be mad! I've got a mother who can give you ten or twelve years. Marguerite's nothing to me. I like her, she's intelligent and attractive, but I don't have to prove anything by trying to make love to her. Come on, love, snap out of it. I don't like to see you like this.

(POPPY *rises and dabs at her face with her handkerchief*)

POPPY. Now I expect I look a sight.

WILF. You always look good to me, love.

(POPPY *moves to the door, hesitates and looks at Wilf*)

POPPY. Are you coming, then?
WILF. I thought you weren't in the mood.
POPPY. I don't want to be on my own, that's all. It doesn't have to be like that every time, does it? Can't we just be together?
WILF. It's asking a lot, Poppy, but I'll try. Just for you.
POPPY. No, don't laugh. It's just that sometimes I get so damned lonely.

(WILF *moves to Poppy and puts his arm around her*)

WILF. Ah, Poppy love, no more daft talk. No more soul-searching, eh?
POPPY. You do love me a little bit, don't you, Wilf?
WILF. You know I do, Poppy. You know I do.

WILF *kisses* POPPY *and in a moment she begins to respond, putting her arms round him and straining him to her as—*

the CURTAIN *falls*

SCENE 3

SCENE—*The same. Evening, a week later.*

When the CURTAIN *rises,* POPPY *is standing at the kitchen table, pouring cocoa into a cup.from a jug. She swallows a couple of aspirin tablets, washes them down with cocoa, then sits in the armchair.* WILF *and* MARGUERITE *enter by the front door.*

WILF. Would you like some cocoa, Marguerite? Poppy should have some on the go.
MARGUERITE. Beer and cocoa. Is that a good mixture?
WILF. It's never done me any harm. (*He goes into the kitchen*)

(MARGUERITE *follows Wilf into the kitchen*)

Ah, Poppy me love! Nothing interesting on television?
POPPY. I don't want to look at it. I've got a splitting head. Have you two been out somewhere?
WILF. Just up to the pub.
POPPY. I thought you'd be working.
WILF. I was earlier, but I gave it up.
POPPY. Something more interesting to do, I suppose?
WILF. Marguerite went to post a letter and I walked on with her for the fresh air. Then we decided to go for a drink. Any further questions?
MARGUERITE (*feeling the slight strain in the atmosphere*) I think I'll be going up.

Wilf. No, don't go, Marguerite. We were wondering if there was any cocoa going, Poppy?
Poppy (*rising*) There's some in that jug. You can see to it yourselves. I'm going to bed. (*She puts a hand up to her head*)
Marguerite. You don't look at all well.
Poppy. I feel as if I've a bout of flu coming on.
Marguerite. Shall I come up with you and see you're all right?
Poppy. I can manage. You stop and get your cocoa.
Wilf. You go with her, Marguerite, and tuck her in.
Poppy. Oh, don't talk so damn silly. Have you had too much to drink or summat?
Wilf. Have a good night's sleep, Poppy love. You'll feel better in the morning.
Poppy. You'll all go without breakfast if I don't. (*She crosses to the door*)
Marguerite. You pour the cocoa, Wilf. I won't be long.
Poppy. You can stay here. I've looked after meself too long to start needing help now.

(Poppy *goes into the hall and exits up the stairs.* Marguerite *sits above the table.* Wilf *goes to the shelves up* c, *collects two mugs, puts them on the table and pours the cocoa*)

Wilf. D'you think she's all right?
Marguerite. I think so. She probably does far too much work. We should have taken her with us to the pub and given her a change.
Wilf. I didn't think of going for a drink, though, till we'd got along the road. You know, you mustn't take her seriously when she's snappy. She's one of the best.
Marguerite. I know. (*She sips her cocoa*) Mmm! This is good.
Wilf. Yes. (*He pauses*) Well, and how's life in the jam trade?
Marguerite. I beg your pardon?
Wilf. The job. How's it going?
Marguerite. I'd ask you, sir, to refrain from adopting that condescending attitude towards the commodities that provide me with my livelihood.
Wilf. Blimey!
Marguerite. And I'd have you know that not only do we fill the family's jampot, we also put the sugar in their tea, the butter on their bread and the currants and raisins in their spotted dog. Moreover, apart from these everyday necessities we handle nuts, dates, figs . . .
Wilf. And all the spices of the Orient.
Marguerite. Oh, it's very romantic. You've no idea. I droop over my invoices and dream of faraway places.
Wilf. Was that one of your people in the pub tonight? The bloke with the crinkly hair and a look of best quality middle-class breeding?

MARGUERITE. As a matter of fact it was the boss's son: Stephen Hollis, heir apparent to the J. G. Hollis fortune.
WILF. He seemed to be very interested in you. Do you see much of him?
MARGUERITE. Not much. It might be more if I encouraged him. But he's really a rather arrogant young man, and anyway, a girl in the office is mad about him. If I showed interest it might complicate matters, even though she doesn't stand a chance.
WILF. Not a hope, eh?
MARGUERITE. I'm afraid not. I can't help feeling sorry for her, though. She eats her heart out in silence and Stephen hardly knows she exists.
WILF. "Stephen", eh?
MARGUERITE. Everybody calls him "Mr Stephen". He's working his way through the firm.
WILF. It reminds me of the American industrialist who called one of his men to him. "Look here," he said, "you came into this firm on the shop floor. In three months you were foreman of your department. In six months you were in charge of a whole section. In another three months you were production manager and three months after that you got a seat on the Board. There hasn't been a success story like yours in the entire history of the company, and now there's a vice-presidency vacant and we're gonna give it to you. Now, whaddya say to that?" "Gee, thanks, Dad!"
MARGUERITE. Don't look now but your prejudices are showing.
WILF. They often do. (*He moves to the fireplace*) It's like I was saying to Poppy the other night . . . (*He stops, remembering the circumstances of that conversation*)
MARGUERITE. What?
WILF (*picking up an ashtray from the mantelpiece*) Oh, just that your upbringing leaves a deep impression. (*He moves to R of the table and puts the ashtray on it*) I don't think you can ever quite emancipate yourself from the first twenty years of your life.
MARGUERITE. Or the first nine, for that matter.
WILF. Was that the time you spent here as a kid?
MARGUERITE. Yes.
WILF. I think the formative years extend well beyond nine, though.
MARGUERITE. Yes, but in my case the life I led after nine was very different from that before.
WILF. You know, what happens to people depends a lot on what kind of people they are. Anyone can get knocked down in the street and be crippled for life, for instance. But it's what they make of it. That's what makes writing novels interesting.
MARGUERITE. My life would make a poor novel. It's been full of things over which I'd no control.
WILF. Yes, but your reactions, they're the important thing. We can always resist events to *some* extent. Look, suppose we were the characters in a novel. Now our sitting here together is the result of

an accident, the accident of our both picking the same house to live in. Here we are, then, where do we go from here?

MARGUERITE. You're the writer, you tell me.

(WILF *sits* R *of the table and leans towards Marguerite*)

WILF. Well, first, there's where we've come from. All right. I come from a mining village in South Yorkshire. I was a wages clerk at a pit. But I wanted to be a writer and I felt inhibited by the life I was leading, so one day I packed my bag and here I am. Now in your case there seems to be a stronger link because you were a child here. Why are you here?

MARGUERITE. Oh—I don't know really why I did come back. I had a definite reason for leaving London—a personal one—but why I chose to come back here—I don't know. I think I had some vague idea of trying to find my bearings where I started.

WILF. What about family?

MARGUERITE. The uncle and aunt I lived with are both dead now.

(*There is a pause.* MARGUERITE *does not enlarge.* WILF *rises, looks at Marguerite for a moment, then goes to the shelves up* C)

WILF. I'm going to poke about for something to eat. There should be a basin of pork dripping somewhere. Yes, here it is. (*He takes a basin of dripping and a sliced loaf from the cupboard and spreads dripping on a few slices of bread*)

MARGUERITE. What made you come here, anyway?

WILF. Well, I'd often thought about leaving home, but it was the day I had my first short story broadcast that decided me. We all sat round the set at home and a daft woman from next door came in and talked all the way through it. And at the end nobody had anything to say. I suddenly realized I couldn't explain what I was trying to do with my writing and I'd just have to get away.

MARGUERITE. I should have thought London was the obvious choice for you.

WILF Oh, this was just far enough for my purpose. The life up here is what I want to write about and I don't see any point in leaving it yet. (*He brings the slices of bread and dripping and puts them on the table*) Here, try some of this. I dug down for the brown bits.

(MARGUERITE *takes a piece of bread and bites from it*)

MARGUERITE. Mmm! It's delicious. Mucky fat. I haven't had any in years.

(WILF *grins*)

What are you smiling at?

WILF (*sitting* R *of the table*) Just the way you use North-country expressions in your posh voice.

MARGUERITE. Oh, dear, is my voice posh?

WILF. Not affected. I didn't mean that. You've no accent, though.

MARGUERITE. I had once, I can tell you. There was a time when I talked really broad. I could swear like a navvy, as well. I was an embarrassment for a long time to my uncle and aunt.

WILF. Where did they live?

MARGUERITE. In Amhurst, a rather snooty country town in Gloucestershire.

WILF. You went to live with them when you left here at—what was it—nine? Were you an orphan?

MARGUERITE. Not exactly. My mother died when I was six, but my father's alive today, for all I know.

WILF. You mean you've no idea where he is?

MARGUERITE. Perhaps here somewhere, I don't know.

WILF. There must be some way you could trace him.

MARGUERITE. I haven't tried. (*She pauses*) I haven't seen him since I was nine. I probably wouldn't know him and I doubt if he'd recognize me.

WILF. You've no brothers or sisters?

MARGUERITE. No. Not now.

(WILF *waits but Marguerite does not continue*)

WILF. Well, what does that mean?

MARGUERITE. I'm sorry. I can't talk about it.

(*The mood of the moment is broken as the front door opens.*

SYLVIA *enters by the front door. She is arguing with a* MAN *on the step outside*)

SYLVIA. I don't care, it's too late. You'll have the house up.

WILF. It sounds as if Sylvia's home early tonight.

MAN (*off*) You promised, you know.

SYLVIA. I never did promise. You'll get me thrown out. You'd better get off home to your wife. And that's enough o' that. Look, come outside and talk quietly, will you?

(SYLVIA *exits by the front door and closes it behind her*)

WILF. Struggling for her honour on the doorstep. I've seen the day when she'd have had him quietly inside and upstairs. Only Poppy laid the law down.

MARGUERITE. Strait-laced, is she, Poppy?

(WILF *looks at Marguerite, wondering if there is any irony in her question*)

WILF. I wouldn't say that. But with Sylvia it's a different one every week. As far as I can make out she's next door to being on the game and Poppy can't afford to let the house get a reputation.

MARGUERITE. What does Sylvia do for a living?

WILF. Waitress, barmaid, millhand, work in factories. (*He rises*) She's done just about everything a woman can do without any

particular training. She's nearly always behind with her rent and
Poppy's threatened many a time to get rid of her.

(Sylvia *enters by the front door, looking slightly dishevelled*)

But every now and then she'll be in funds and pay some of it off.
And Poppy's soft as a brush, really. She thinks if she chucks Sylvia
out it'll help her along the downward path.

(Sylvia *opens the kitchen door*)

Sylvia. Oh, you two having a nice cosy supper by yourselves, are
you? Where's Poppy?
Wilf. In bed. She wasn't feeling too good.
Sylvia. That's all right, then. I thought she might have heard
that performance at t'door.
Wilf. What performance was that?
Sylvia. Don't tell me you didn't hear anything. I was near
shouting me flamin' head off at the end. Bloody men! (*She moves to
the table where she supports herself with one hand while she slips off one of
her shoes and rubs her foot*) They buy you a couple o' shorts and think
they own you. (*She glares at Marguerite*) Best piece of advice I can
give you is don't let 'em get you in a car. Not a Mini, anyway.
I'd never ha' got out o' that one if he hadn't thought he was going
straight upstairs.
Marguerite. I think I can take care of myself.
Sylvia. Aye, don't we all? Married, that one. They usually are.
They're worse than the single ones. Allus after a bit o' novelty.
(*She sits* l *of the table and kicks off her other shoe*) Oh, don't start thinking
I'm a prude or owt like that. I like a bit o' fun and I've had me share
in me time. After all, life's short, in't it? We're here today and God
knows where tomorrow. But I am a bit particular and it's come to
a pretty pass where you can't exchange a friendly word with a feller
wi'out him expecting you to strip off for him. I hope I'm not em-
barrassing you, love, talking like this in front of Wilf here——
Wilf (*sitting* r *of the table*) Don't mind me.
Sylvia. —but a bit o' plain speaking's very useful now and
again, I allus think; and it's a job if a lass can't take a bit o' good
advice from an older woman. (*She sniggers*) Hark at me! Older
woman! I wouldn't talk like that in front of everybody. (*She takes
her compact and lipstick from her handbag, tidies her hair and attends to her
make-up*) How old would you say I was love, anyway?
Marguerite. It's hard to say. I mean, appearances are decep-
tive.
Sylvia. I know they are. That's why I wanted you to guess.
Wilf. Don't worry, Sylvia; nobody in his right mind would put
you at more than forty-six.
Sylvia. Forty-six! I'll have you know I've yet to see thirty.
Wilf. Yes, the second time round.
Sylvia. What d'you mean, "the second time round"? You're

in a right clever mood tonight, aren't you? What's up, haven't you been getting any co-operation either?

WILF. Cut that out, Sylvia. I was only pulling your leg.

SYLVIA. Well, try somebody else's leg. You've no need to come the high and mighty sarcasm in front of her because you're no angel, an' neither is Poppy. There's things about her that *you* don't know.

WILF (*rising*) I said stop it! You want to remember who your friends are. That sort of talk'll get you nowhere but out in the street with your bag in your hand.

SYLVIA (*becoming maudlin*) I know, I know. You don't have to tell me what sort o' future I've got. It's you men what get the best out o' life. Take what you want an' go marching on to the next stop.

WILF. You know too many of the wrong kind. (*He picks up Sylvia's shoes*)

SYLVIA. Is there a right kind? Oh, aye, some of 'em might look a bit different an' talk a bit different, but there's not much difference when you dig down a bit. I could tell you some tales.

WILF. But not tonight, Sylvia, eh? (*He hands the shoes to Sylvia*)

SYLVIA (*rising*) No, I'm off to bed. Get an early night for a change.

MARGUERITE (*pointing*) You'll be losing your brooch.

(SYLVIA *looks at the cheap brooch hanging by its pin from her coat and pins its back in place*)

SYLVIA. Lucky it's not broken. That feller again. As many hands as a flamin' octopus. All over you, they are. (*Her glance falls on the plate*) Ey, is that dripping?

WILF. Yes, want some?

SYLVIA. If it's going begging, I don't mind. All I've had since me tea's a bag of crisps an' a couple of cheese straws. (*She takes a couple of pieces of bread and makes a sandwich. She bites from it and turns at the door to speak with her mouth full in a "posh" voice*) The bathroom will be occupied for the next twenty minutes while I have my bubble bath. I'll leave the door unlocked in case you feel like coming up an' scrubbing me back for me.

WILF. I'll think about it.

SYLVIA (*amiably*) I bet you would an' all. Well, don't leave it too long else the water 'ull go cold an' all me bubbles 'ull burst.

(SYLVIA *goes into the hall and exits up the stairs.* WILF *closes the door behind Sylvia then moves to* L *of Marguerite*)

WILF. Don't mind her. She has to issue these random invitations to keep her spirits up. (*He yawns hugely and stretches his arms*) Ugh! First beer makes me feel amorous, and then it puts me to sleep.

MARGUERITE. That's a useful thing for a girl to know.

WILF. Hmmm?

MARGUERITE. It could help her to plan her tactics.

WILF. Defence or attack?

MARGUERITE. Military secret.

WILF. I was just talking, y'know.

MARGUERITE. So was I.

WILF. Well, I'll tell you. If ever I do make a pass at you—and if I don't it won't be because I don't think you're a very attractive girl—if I do, I'll do you the honour of being stone-cold sober at the time.

MARGUERITE. Exit attractive girl in confusion. Leaving pompous young male in command of the stage and his self-esteem.

WILF. You'd better go to bed.

MARGUERITE. And wedge a chair under the door-handle?

WILF. If it'll make you any happier. (*He yawns*) Gosh, when I go I go all at once.

MARGUERITE (*rising*) Anyway, thank you for this evening. I've enjoyed it very much.

(WILF *transfers the crockery, etc., from the table to the shelves up* C)

WILF. We must have a real evening out sometime.

MARGUERITE. I'd like that. But you'd better be getting on top of that novel.

WILF (*picking up Marguerite's scarf*) Yeh, I suppose so. All play and no work makes no Jack . . . Or something.

(WILF *and* MARGUERITE *go into the hall.* MARGUERITE, *at the foot of the stairs, stretches out her arm for her scarf. At the same moment* WILF, *as though on impulse, reaches out and takes her hand. It is all done very lightly.* MARGUERITE *looks steadily at Wilf for a moment as though in slight surprise, then withdraws her hand*)

I'll see you in the morning, then.

MARGUERITE. Yes. Good night.

(MARGUERITE *exits up the stairs.* WILF *goes into the kitchen and looks into space for a moment*)

WILF. You stupid nit! You nearly made a pass after all.

CURTAIN

ACT II

SCENE—*The same. Evening, a week later.*

When the CURTAIN *rises,* POPPY *is in the kitchen, ironing at an ironing-board. The creel has been lowered.* WILF *is in his room, seated at his type-writer. The sound of a high-powered car arriving and stopping is heard.* WILF *rises, moves to the window, opens the curtains a crack and peers out.* SYLVIA *enters down the stairs, dressed for going out. She is in a minor state of excitement. She taps on* WILF's *door, opens it and looks in. She enters, moves, and stands beside* WILF, *craning her neck to see out of the window.*

SYLVIA. Has he come for Marguerite?

WILF. Well, it's not one of *your* boy friends, is it, Sylvia?

SYLVIA. I can see the day when somebody calls for me in a car like that.

WILF (*half to himself*) I might have known he'd drive a Jaguar. I could have guessed.

SYLVIA. Is that Marguerite coming down? (*She hurries into the hall*)

(MARGUERITE *enters down the stairs. She wears a light raincoat over a semi-formal black dress*)

Oh, Marguerite, I saw the car. Isn't it posh? Do you think you'll be going through the city centre?

MARGUERITE. I think we're going the other way.

SYLVIA. Just my luck. Well, I'll run for me bus.

(WILF *comes into the hall.*
SYLVIA *exits by the front door*)

WILF (*calling after Sylvia*) And have a good look at him at the same time. (*To Marguerite*) I assume that it is Mr Stephen Hollis?

MARGUERITE. Right first time.

WILF. You said the other night you hardly knew him.

MARGUERITE. It was true. This is the first time he's asked me out.

WILF. Not that it's any of my business.

MARGUERITE. You said it—not me.

WILF. Are you going anywhere nice?

MARGUERITE. To a dinner-dance at the *Crossed Keys*, wherever that might be.

WILF. Somewhere out in the industrialists' belt. Still, variety's the spice of life. When I take you out it'll be bingo and a fish and fourpenn'orth from Wilson's Deep Sea Fisheries.

MARGUERITE. And I'll wear my best hair-curlers.

(MARGUERITE *exits by the front door.* WILF *goes into his room and cannot resist going to the window to watch the departure. The sound is heard of the car starting up and driving away.* WILF *goes to his table, picks up the growing pile of typescript that is his novel and riffles through it with satisfaction. He puts the typescript down, switches off the desk lamp, and goes into the hall, switching off the lights in his room as he leaves, then enters the kitchen*)

WILF. Poppy, my love, you've got a genius in the house.

POPPY. Well, don't let 'em get to know at the Town Hall or they'll put me rates up.

WILF. In a hundred years' time they'll be putting a plaque by the front door saying "Wilf Cotton, author, lived here". (*Playfully*) And learned dons will be investigating this period in my life and trying to find out if the mysterious Mrs Poppy Swallow was any more to the struggling young genius than the temporary provider of his board and lodging.

POPPY. Never mind. We shall all be past caring. You've knocked off early tonight, haven't you?

WILF. Because I've broken through, Poppy. I've been sweating over it for a fortnight and now I've broken through. I thought I'd stop while it was going well, then I can bash straight into it tomorrow I'll take time to get it down, but I can see it now and it's going to be good.

POPPY. There's a couple of your shirts and some clean underwear on the airer. You'll manage for a bit longer now.

WILF. You know, you're a bloody marvel, Poppy. Only the other night you were dead on your feet and now you're working away as if nothing had happened.

POPPY. If I stop everything stops.

WILF. I was thinking it might be nice to walk up to the *Tower* and get cosily drunk.

POPPY. And what then, when we've got cosily drunk?

WILF. Well, with some people it's an end in itself, but with us it could lead to other things.

POPPY. That's what I thought. Anyway, I don't feel like going out tonight.

WILF. Pity.

POPPY. There should be a couple of bottles in the scullery cupboard, though, if you'd like a drink here.

WILF (*moving to the scullery door*) Poppy the great provider.

POPPY. Bring one for me. I'm feeling a bit parched.

(WILF *exits to the scullery*)

WILF (*off*) Where's the opener?

POPPY. On a hook, over the sink.

WILF (*off*) Got it.

(WILF *enters from the scullery carrying two half-pint bottles of beer and two tumblers, which he puts on the table*)

Now you're going to sit down and drink this. Get the load off your feet.

POPPY. Pour it out. I've nearly finished.

(WILF *pours the beer*)

Ironing. There seems no end to it sometimes.

WILF. Wait till the novel's a best seller. I'll buy you a machine.

POPPY (*dryly*) Aye, with a plaque on it.

(WILF *laughs.* POPPY *sits* R *of the table.* WILF *hands Poppy her drink*)

WILF (*raising his glass*) Cheers.

POPPY (*raising her glass*) All the best, love. Who was that young feller who called for Marguerite tonight?

(*They drink. During the following speeches* WILF *unplugs the iron, puts it in the hearth, then folds the ironing-board and stands it in the corner up* L. *He then raises the creel*)

WILF. That was Stephen Hollis, Crown Prince of the J. G. Hollis empire. "Mister Stephen" to the family retainers.

POPPY. He looked a very presentable young chap.

WILF. He should with his backing.

POPPY. You sound a bit sour. Has he put your nose out of joint?

WILF. She can go out with whom she likes, but the casual arrogance of blokes like Stephen Hollis makes my back hair bristle.

POPPY. I think you're just plain jealous.

WILF. Oh, knock it off, Poppy. We've had all this out before.

POPPY. I don't say you know it yourself, but that's what I think it is.

WILF. You seem set on conjuring something up between Marguerite and me.

POPPY. She's a lovely girl.

WILF. I'm not saying she isn't. But apart from her not being interested in me, lovely girls want wedding rings and homes and kids. They festoon a man with responsibilities, and right now I want responsibilities like I want two broken legs. I've got things to do. (*He sits* L *of the table*)

POPPY. A woman can often help a man to make his way.

WILF. *You* help me, Poppy. You give me all I want from a woman.

POPPY. And you think it'll be there till you don't need it any more?

WILF. You're twisting it, Poppy. You know I've never demanded anything. I take what you give me and give what I can in return.

POPPY. The world's full of men who'd like an arrangement like that.

WILF. Well, of course it is. D'you think I don't know how lucky I am? It's not a question of measuring who's getting the best of the bargain. You don't seem to see, Poppy, that as soon as you start talking about it like this, analysing it, resentment creeps in and it's spoilt.

POPPY. Oh, I see, all right.

WILF (*gently*) Why couldn't it have stayed as it was, Poppy? Why let all this talk in to spoil it?

POPPY. I've told you before, we're human beings, not animals. We've got to talk. We don't just work by instinct. We've got to think things out and find reasons.

WILF. Our reason was that we got on well together and liked to make love.

POPPY. Yes.

WILF. And now it's not good enough. (*He pauses*) Poppy, why haven't you ever got married again?

POPPY. Who'd want me at my age?

WILF (*rising*) Don't talk wet, Poppy. Any number of men. God knows, you could find some steady-living widower with his family grown up and give him a whole new lease of life.

POPPY. Sexy Poppy, the old men's darling.

WILF. That's not what I meant. You should be thinking about it, though. You've still got a lot of future left and you don't want to spend it on your own.

POPPY. Happen I won't.

WILF. Would you marry me if I asked you to?

POPPY. No, 'course I wouldn't. I wouldn't even if I could. And I can't. There's something I've never told you, but you'll have to know now. I've got a husband already.

(*There is a pause as this information gets home to* WILF)

WILF (*finally*) Well, you kept that little bit of information to yourself, didn't you?

POPPY. There was never any need to tell you before. I haven't seen Alf for years and I hardly expected to hear from him again. For all I knew he was dead. Then I got a letter from him this morning.

WILF. Why should he suddenly write to you now?

POPPY. Perhaps he's got a conscience about the way he treated me. Perhaps he's just feeling lonely and sorry for himself, because he's got nowhere to go. He's due to come out of prison, you see.

WILF. Prison!

POPPY. Aye, prison. He says he got in with a bad crowd down in London and got three years for robbery with violence. You may as well read it for yourself. It's up there on the mantelshelf.

(WILF *moves to the fireplace, takes a letter from behind the clock on the mantelpiece, opens it and reads it*)

He says himself 'at he can't blame me if I won't take him back,
but he's coming out in a few days and he's got nowhere to go.

Wilf. He *sounds* repentant enough.

Poppy. Oh, he'll be repentant enough now. He probably cries
himself to sleep at nights thinking of all the wrong he's done me
and imagining the grand reunion. Alf always had a sentimental
streak a yard wide.

(Wilf *hands Poppy the letter in silence*)

(*She gazes at the letter for a moment*) It hasn't upset you, has it?

Wilf (*sickened*) Oh, bloody hell, Poppy!

Poppy. You said yourself it couldn't go on for ever. It'd have to
end sometime.

Wilf. I know.

Poppy. You mean you wanted it to be you who'd end it. You'd
be the one who'd walk out one day and not come back.

Wilf. How did it all happen? Why did you marry somebody like
that?

Poppy. Oh, it was one of those quick war-time marriages. He
was in the army and he went abroad soon after. It was hard to
weigh a man up in those days. You put so much down to war.
When he came back he settled down for a while and then the restless
side of him began to show through. He began to drift from job to
job and he was drinking more than was good for him. He was very
nasty in drink. He landed in court once for clouting a chap at work
and that sobered him up for a bit. Then it all started again—losing
jobs, drinking, carrying on with other women. We had blazing
rows all the time. In the end he walked out and went off with his
fancy woman. I've never heard of him again—apart from a few
vague stories from his brother when he was up here. Then this letter
came. Nobody knew me round these parts and when they took me
for a widow I let them go on believing it.

Wilf. You never tried to divorce him?

Poppy. No, I never did.

Wilf. You know that once he gets inside this house you may lose
your chance?

Poppy. Yes, I can see that.

Wilf. Well, for God's sake, Poppy, send him away. It's plain
what kind of a man he is. Don't let him get inside. Now's your
chance to be free of him for good.

Poppy. No, I can't do that. He's in trouble, with nobody to turn
to. I've got to give him a chance to show he's changed. Besides, he
always had a way with him. (*She looks away*)

Wilf (*very sorry for himself*) Well, that sounds all right. That's fine.
That's just fine.

CURTAIN

SCENE 2

SCENE—*The same. Later the same evening.*

When the CURTAIN *rises,* WILF *and* HARRY *are sitting silently in Wilf's room, which is lit only by the firelight and the table lamp* L. HARRY *is seated in the chair* C *and* WILF *is seated in the armchair* L. MARGUERITE *enters by the front door and looks back over her shoulder. The roar of a powerful car is heard as it moves off along the street.* MARGUERITE *closes the door and lingers in the hall. She looks at Wilf's door and lifts her hand as though to knock, then lets it fall again.* POPPY *enters the kitchen from the scullery. She is wearing a quilted dressing-gown over her nightdress. She crosses the kitchen and goes into the hall, switching out the kitchen light as she does so.* MARGUERITE *is startled by Poppy's sudden appearance.*

POPPY. Oh, it's you, Marguerite. I thought I heard a car go off.

MARGUERITE. I thought everybody was in bed except Wilf. I noticed his light was still on.

POPPY. He might be up for a while yet. His brother turned up not long ago.

MARGUERITE. Was Wilf expecting him?

POPPY. No, the door bell rang and there he was. Still, Wilf's got over it. He's had one or two surprises tonight. Have you had a nice time?

MARGUERITE. Lovely, thanks.

POPPY. Sure you're all right? You look a bit pale.

MARGUERITE. I've got a headache. Too much wine, probably.

POPPY. You can be forgiven once in a while. Have you got some aspirin? Take a couple. They'll help you to get a good night's rest. Would you like me to bring you a cup of cocoa? It won't take a minute.

(MARGUERITE *is inordinately touched by* POPPY's *kindness and turns her face away*)

(*Softly*) Ey, you haven't been having any trouble with that young feller, have you?

MARGUERITE. Oh, no, that's the last thing. Everything clean-cut and gentlemanly. He says the prospects for a girl like me are unlimited, and there was a moment tonight when I felt sure that if I played my cards right I could marry him.

POPPY. And that wouldn't be what you want?

MARGUERITE (*near to tears*) I don't know what I do want. I don't know who I am or where I'm going. He said perhaps I'd like to go to his house for supper one evening and meet his family, and all I felt was panic, just cold panic. You mustn't mind me. I'm just a damned cry-baby.

C

POPPY. There's nowt wrong with a woman having a cry now and again. It's her safety valve.

(POPPY *puts her arm around* MARGUERITE *and leads her up the stairs*)

You come on up to my room for five minutes. We'll have a little chat.

(MARGUERITE *and* POPPY *exit up the stairs.* WILF *rises and switches on the wall-brackets.* HARRY *takes cigarettes from his pocket and offers one to* WILF, *who refuses it with a wave of his hand.* HARRY *lights a cigarette for himself*)

WILF. You say mam doesn't know where you are?

HARRY. No, I told you. The bike's laid up. I went into Calderford and had a couple of drinks. Then I saw a bus coming this way and hopped on to it.

WILF. She'll wonder what's happened to you when she finds your bed empty in the morning.

HARRY. I can't help that. I had to talk to somebody, and not in Bronhill, either. It's too good a tale to keep to yourself. Mention it to the wrong bloke and it'll be all over the village in twenty-four hours. Anyway, me mam'll know about it now—or some of it—if he's kept his word.

WILF (*moving to* R *of Harry*) D'you really think he meant it?

HARRY. He meant it when he said it, all right. If wishing could've done it I'd've dropped dead on the spot. God, but I've not seen anybody as mad as that in a long time.

WILF. Y'know, I don't like to say this, old lad, but I did warn you what sort of a bloke he was.

HARRY. Well, I mean, Wilf, any bloke would ha' been mad, wouldn't he? You can't blame him for that.

WILF. I know. But another bloke might have settled for taking a swing at you. Trust Ronnie to think of bringing a charge.

HARRY (*rising and moving to the fireplace*) Aye, and another bloke might ha' got round to wondering afterwards just how much encouragement *she'd* given. (*He flicks his cigarette into the ashtray on the mantelpiece*)

WILF. Well, he's had time to think it over a bit now. Maybe it's done some good.

HARRY. I dunno. I've been thinking about it all last night an' today. Me mind's in a whirl.

WILF. Just how far had you got when he turned up?

HARRY. All I can say is it's a bloody good job he wasn't ten minutes later, that's all.

WILF. You say you didn't know Ronnie was out?

HARRY. No. (*He sits on the right end of the bed*) June answered the door and she didn't tell me till I'd got right inside that Ronnie was away on business and wouldn't be back that night. There wasn't any need for me to rush off, though, was there, she said. I could sit down for five minutes, now I was there.

WILF (*sitting on the desk chair*) What time was this?

HARRY. Oh, about eight. I was glad the telly was on because I didn't really know what to talk to her about. She never says a lot when Ronnie's there and this was the first time I'd really been on me own with her. (*He glances at his watch*) Is it really twenty past twelve, already?

WILF (*looking at his watch*) Twenty-five past, I make it.

HARRY (*rising and moving to the fireplace*) You're sure your landlady doesn't mind me kipping down here? (*He stubs out his cigarette in the ashtray on the mantepiece*)

WILF. No, she gave us the blankets, didn't she?

HARRY. Aye, she seemed all right about it. I don't want to queer your pitch, though.

WILF. Get on with your tale. There must have been some kind of conversation.

HARRY. Oh, you couldn't call it conversation. She'd say summat about Ronnie while the commercials were on, or ask me summat about meself. She asked about you one time; how you were getting on. We smoked a lot. I'd have one of her cigs then she'd have one of mine.

WILF. Did you get the impression she was nervous at all? You know, a bit excited because you were on your own together?

HARRY. No, I don't think I did. (*He sits on the right end of the bed*) She said things about the programmes while they were on. There was a play and she made remarks about the characters like a kid might do. "He's a cheeky devil" and "she'd better watch out". Things like that.

WILF. Could be she's not very bright.

HARRY. Tell you the truth, I don't think she is. 'Course it never was her brains I was interested in.

(WILF *laughs*)

It's all right for you, mate; you're not in this lot.

WILF. Sorry. Carry on.

HARRY. Well, we sat like that till about ten, then she said she'd make some coffee.

WILF. I suppose by this time you were thinking how to make a pass at her?

HARRY. I'd been thinking about it all night, man. I didn't know when a chance like this might come up again. No, things started moving a bit when she brought the supper in. I thought she was just making coffee but she came in with a tray of sandwiches and biscuits. She said her and Ronnie often had supper off a tray like that and I said summat about the joys of married life. Then she said had I never thought about trying it and I said I expected I'd get round to it one day but I wasn't thinking about it serious yet. So she said it was all right for men, they could go around having as much fun as they liked but when they got married they expected the girl to be absolutely untouched. I said I didn't think all men were like that and anyway, lots of lasses didn't bother much about that kind of thing until they did get wed. "Perhaps they don't," she said, "but some men are very good at persuading them." "Oh, you've got to use a bit of persuasion," I said. "That's part of the game." "I'll bet you're good at it, too," she says. Well, you can imagine how I was feeling by this time.

WILF. I think so.

HARRY. I said I'd had me moments, like, but I didn't want her to think I was out with women every night. Oh, no, she said, she didn't think that, but when you'd been married a while you forgot what it was like when you were single and men were attentive and paid you compliments. In fact, she said, even though you were perfectly happy with your husband, there were times when you thought it'd be a pleasant change if another chap did make advances.

WILF. And that was where you went into action.

HARRY. Aye, it was. The next thing I knew we were sprawling across the settee and she was ruffling me hair while I kissed her. She said, "You've been wanting to do this a long time, haven't you?" I said how did you know, and she said women could always tell. So we went into another clinch. She didn't hold me off at all and when I thought it was time I started to unfasten her blouse. Hey, are you getting a second-hand thrill out of all this?

WILF (grinning) I'm a bit envious.

HARRY. You won't be in a minute. I'm sorry to disappoint you but there's not much more to it. The telly was still playing and we were so busy with what we were doing, not expecting anybody, that we never heard Ronnie come up the path. The first thing we know is the back door opening and him shouting hello. Two seconds after Ronnie shouts June's pushing me off and shouting herself. "Get off, get off, leave me alone!" And she's on her feet, breathing heavy, her face red, her hair mussed up, and somehow her blouse is torn. And Ronnie's standing in the doorway gawping at us. He can't speak for a minute, but June's saying plenty. Thank God Ronnie's back, he's just come at the right time. Another minute later and she doesn't know what might have happened. (He rises and moves above the bed) Then she turns away and pulls her blouse together and reckons to be sobbing. Ronnie drops his case and starts on me. His face is red at first and then it goes as white as lard. I'm a dirty sneaking bastard, supposed to be a friend of the family and the minute his back's turned I sneak in there and molest his wife. And so on, while I gather me wits and try to get over the shock of him coming home and the way June's turned round on me. I ask him if he really thinks I forced her to it, and tell him so he's caught us having a cuddle but there wasn't any more to it than that and she wasn't pushing me off a minute since. Then June turns round on me and calls me a rotten liar and she acts the part so well I can nearly believe her meself. All this time I'm keeping me eye on Ronnie because I'm expecting him to come for me. But he doesn't. He's kinda rooted to the spot with rage. Some blokes would punch me in the face, he says, but that's too good for a two-faced bastard like me. He'll show me up good and proper. He'll lay a charge against me for criminal assault. By the time he's finished my name'll stink with every decent man and woman in the village. (*He lifts his hands expressively*) Cor, what a bitch!

WILF. Come to think of it, you can't expect her to admit straight out that she'd led you on.

HARRY. No, but it's a bit thick coming the assault business.

WILF. There was no whisper of it about at work yesterday?

HARRY. No, and I was listening for it, believe me. You do think I can be had up for it, then?

WILF. I don't think there's much doubt about that. If Master Ronnie and his missis really feel malicious they can make things very hot for you.

HARRY. But, I mean, I only kissed her and put me hand inside her blouse and she practically invited me to do that.

WILF. But that's not what she's saying now, is it?

HARRY. What can they do to me, then?

WILF. Oh, I don't know. Mebbe only a fine or probation. I'd say a lot depends on how bad Ronnie paints the picture. Anyway, it won't happen to you.

HARRY (*gloomily*) I wish I'd your confidence, mate.

WILF. Well, you should have. Have you forgotten you've got a joker up your sleeve that neither of them knows about?

HARRY. What's that?

WILF. That photograph of June in the raw.

HARRY. Oh, that.

WILF. Yes, that. Don't tell me you've thrown it away.

HARRY. No. I've got it in me wallet.

WILF. That's okay, then.

HARRY. I don't see what use it is, though.

WILF. Use your loaf, man. Think.

HARRY. You mean because she's had her photo taken in her pants she can't be assaulted.

WILF (*rising*) I mean that if June thought Ronnie was going to get to know about that photo she might talk him out of going ahead with his revenge. Or if Ronnie saw it he might think that June could have given you some encouragement after all. And if the worst came to the worse I'd say it was a relevant bit of evidence, wouldn't you? If nothing else it would show that Mrs Ronnie Betley isn't quite all she seems and you're not quite the rogue they're making you out to be.

HARRY. You're a devil when you get going, aren't you?

WILF. It all depends how hard I'm pushed. (*He picks up two folded blankets from the bed and puts them on the chair* C) These two chairs won't be as comfortable as a bed, but you'll manage.

HARRY. I'm tired enough to sleep on a clothes-line tonight.

WILF. First thing in the morning I'll go home and tell mum

where you are and see the Betleys as well. Let's hope it won't be too late, that's all.

HARRY. Oh, hell! I don't know where I am with you. One minute you're saying it'll be all right and the next you're on about it being too late.

WILF. You know, you're like a bloody little boy, Harry. You've got to face the facts. All my life, Harry, you've been there, three years older than me, the leader, the bloke who knew what was what. The man who did a man's work while his brother pushed a pen and messed about with writing in his spare time. Now here you are, coming to see me because there's no-one else you can talk to. Coming to me for advice and help.

HARRY. Don't rub it in.

WILF. No, I like it, Harry. If nothing else comes out of this I'll always be pleased you came to me.

HARRY. You've got all the flamin' brains in the family. You might as well use 'em for summat useful now and again.

WILF (*sarcastically*) Aye, playing Miss Lonelyhearts to you. (*He moves to the fireplace*)

(HARRY *pulls a face at Wilf, moves to the door and opens it*)

HARRY. Where is it?

WILF. To the left on the first landing. Don't wake the house up.

(HARRY *goes into the hall and exits up the stairs*)

(*He strikes a pose*) "Dear Worried Blue Eyes, there is nothing unusual in your feelings, which are perfectly normal—for a sex maniac."

WILF *grins, takes a pillow from his bed and throws it into the armchair* c *as*—

the CURTAIN *falls*

ACT III

SCENE—*The same. The following evening.*

When the CURTAIN *rises, the lights and fire are on in* Wilf's *room, but the window curtains are not yet closed.* HARRY, *in his shirt-sleeves, is seated in the armchair* L, *leafing through a magazine without really reading it. His jacket is on the bed. There is an opened bottle of whisky and two tumblers on the table.* HARRY *throws the magazine aside, glances at his watch and rises.* SYLVIA *enters down the stairs.* HARRY *pours himself a drink. As he does so, something outside the window catches his attention and he goes quickly into the hall as* SYLVIA *reaches the bottom of the stairs.*

SYLVIA. Oh! Good evening.
HARRY. Er—good evening.

(WILF *enters by the front door. He wears a raincoat*)

SYLVIA. I haven't seen you playing the piano at the *White Bull*, have I?
WILF. You've got him mixed up with two other fellers, Sylvia.
SYLVIA. He is like him, though. Well, my mistake. Ta ra, all.

(SYLVIA *exits by the front door.* WILF *and* HARRY *go into* Wilf's *room*)

HARRY. Who's that, then?
WILF. Oh, that's Sylvia. It's a pity you didn't make your pass at her. (*He removes his coat*)
HARRY. Why, is she available? (*He collects his drink*)
WILF. A bit too much so, from all accounts. (*He throws his raincoat across the bed*)
HARRY (*sitting in the armchair* L) You took your time, didn't you? I was expecting you to ring up.
WILF. Were you?
HARRY. Well, there was no flamin' need to keep me in suspense, was there?
WILF. Perhaps I didn't want to give you bad news.
HARRY. It's like that, is it?
WILF. It's neither good nor bad. I haven't seen him.
HARRY. Oh, God, you mean you couldn't find him?
WILF. That's right. I hung about till I couldn't wait any longer. Then I put a note through his letter-box asking him to phone me. (*He flops into the armchair* C) Gosh, I'm tired now.
HARRY. Does me mother know owt?
WILF. Apparently not. He seems to have kept it all pretty quiet so far.

HARRY. Well, that's summat to be thankful for. What do we do now, then?

WILF. Wait, I suppose. (*He looks at the whisky bottle*) Are you on the hard stuff?

HARRY. I thought we might have summat to celebrate.

WILF. Sorry.

HARRY. Oh, I reckon you've done your best. D'you want a spot?

WILF. No, not just now. What have you been doing all day, then, apart from tippling?

HARRY. Biting me finger-nails. Poppy gave me a grand dinner and didn't ask any questions. She's a bit of all right, that one.

WILF. So you've said before.

HARRY. Aye, well, it's what I think. Then I had a nap this afternoon and read a bit. I allus did like reading. 'S'matter of fact I had a look at that book you're writing. When you gunna finish it?

WILF. When I can find time off from looking after other people's affairs.

HARRY. You want to get stuck into it. It's not bad at all. A bit warm in parts.

WILF (*affecting not to understand*) Warm?

HARRY. Y'know—the sexy bits.

WILF (*loftily*) I take it there was nothing you'd have found offensive in somebody else's book?

HARRY. Oh, no. You know me. I'm as broadminded as they come. I've read some pretty crude stuff in me time. Not that yours is like that. Oh, no, it's very good.

WILF. Well, that's all right, then. (*He pauses*) I'm hungry.

HARRY. I'm a bit peckish meself.

WILF. There's a fish and chip shop on the main road. What about popping up and fetching some for us.

HARRY (*rising*) Let's both go and have a pint at the same time. (*He crosses and puts his glass on the table*)

WILF. I'm a bit done in.

HARRY. You'll feel better when you've had a pint. Why don't we ask Poppy to go with us?

WILF (*not seriously*) You haven't been up to anything with Poppy, have you?

HARRY. You're a suspicious bastard, aren't you? (*Slyly*) Anyway, she's not like that, is she?

WILF (*blandly*) No, she isn't.

HARRY. Well, then. If I didn't know you better I'd be wondering if you weren't up to something with her yourself.

WILF. But you do know me better, don't you?

HARRY. I'm not sure. You're full of surprises.

WILF. Who isn't? (*He rises*) Come on, we'll go on our own.

HARRY. Just as you like.

(WILF *sees something through the window*)

WILF. Hey, isn't that Ronnie Betley's car?

HARRY. Where? (*He moves to the window and looks out*) What the hell's he doing here?

WILF. I don't know, but you'd better scarper into the kitchen while I see what he wants.

(HARRY *grabs his jacket, goes into the hall, then into the kitchen where he remains quietly in the dark.* WILF *goes into the hall. The door bell rings.* WILF *opens the front door.*

RONNIE BETLEY *is on the doorstep. He is a dapper man of about thirty*)

Now then, Ronnie. This is a surprise visit. Come in.

RONNIE (*stepping into the hall*) I wanted to see that brother of yours. I've a few things to say to him.

WILF. I'm afraid you've missed him. (*He closes the front door*)

RONNIE. He's been here, then?

WILF. Yes, he's been. Come on in here. (*He leads the way into his room*)

(RONNIE *follows* WILF *into the room*)

Would you like a drink?

RONNIE (*reluctantly*) Go on, then.

(WILF *pours a whisky for Ronnie and hands it to him*)

He'd tell you all about it, then?

WILF. He gave me his version of what happened. According to him there was some mention of bringing a charge.

RONNIE. That's right.

WILF. It struck me that he must have misunderstood in the confusion. You know—misheard.

RONNIE. He heard, all right.

WILF. You really did threaten to have him charged?

RONNIE. That's right.

(WILF *appears to consider this, crosses and sits in the armchair* L)

WILF. Well, there's no denying that Harry was in the wrong to some extent—but a charge. That's going a bit far, isn't it?

RONNIE. To some extent, y'say? That bloody brother of yours has shown himself as the biggest bastard for miles around. He's come to my house practically every week and he's always been made welcome. We've treated him as a friend of the family and June and I have always said what a grand bloke he was and wondered when he was going to find a nice young woman and settle down.

(WILF *nods gravely at this image of wholesome friendship*)

And then what? When I'd trust him with anything I'd got, what does he do? The first time he finds June on her own he tries to rape her.

WILF. Oh, come now, Ronnie. That's a bit strong, surely.

RONNIE. Strong, y'say? The only bloody thing that stopped him was me walking in when I did.

WILF. I should've thought June was capable of holding him off, if she wanted to.

RONNIE. Now, just a minute, mate. This is my wife we're talking about. What d' you mean "if she wanted to"?

WILF (*innocently*) Just a slip of the tongue, Ronnie. No offence meant.

RONNIE. I'd like you to know how much this has upset June. It's a wonder she hasn't had a breakdown.

WILF. I'm sorry about that. Any decent, unsuspecting woman would be upset. And honestly, in your shoes, Ronnie, I'd think hard before I dragged it on and made it worse for her.

RONNIE. What d'you mean?

WILF. Well, if you bring a charge it means her going through the ordeal of testifying about what happened—and in detail. Think of the publicity, as well. I wouldn't want a wife of mine to have her name bandied about in every pub in the village.

RONNIE. No, and you don't want Harry's name bandied about, either, do you?

WILF. Of course not. But you know how it is for a man. They'll nudge one another and wink and say hard lines, he didn't get away with it, and they wouldn't mind having a crack at the same target themselves.

RONNIE (*violently*) Now, look here . . .

WILF. Don't kid yourself about it, Ronnie. They all know June's an attractive woman. You know what their minds are like. They'll tear her to pieces. They'll say she must have given him some encouragement because haven't all three of you been as thick as thieves for months? Why was Harry always at your house? Because June must have been making up to him when you weren't looking. (*He rises*) And then there's you. It'll be bad enough for Harry but he can always clear out when it's all over. He's a nobody. But you're not a nobody. Everybody knows you. They look up to you and the men respect you. But they work hard and they play hard and they know how to handle their women. And a man that can't handle his woman without calling in the police . . . (*He stops with an expressive shrug*)

RONNIE (*after a pause*) Well, I thought I was a good talker, but you're a bloody expert yourself. Got another drink?

WILF. Help yourself.

(RONNIE *goes to the table, refills his glass then sits in the armchair* C)

RONNIE. How many people has Harry told about this?

WILF. Only me. And you've got my solemn assurance that it won't get out from us.

RONNIE (*snorting*) Your solemn assurance. That's rich. Thank you very much. You don't have to be reckon to be protecting us when you're only looking after your precious brother.

Wilf. You're all three in it together. What affects one affects you all.

Ronnie. I don't know what the hell you're talking about. To listen to you you'd think we were accomplices in something when the truth is we're the injured party and it's Harry who's in trouble.

Wilf (*moving to L of Ronnie*) Is June ready to swear in court that she gave him no encouragement, nor the slightest sign that she wouldn't mind if he made a pass at her?

Ronnie. She's ready to swear to the truth. And before you go any further along that line, mate, remember what I told you—it's my wife we're talking about.

Wilf. I'm only trying to show you what will happen. Harry won't give in without a fight and his lawyer's sure to try to discredit June. The world's full of stupid people who'll cut off their nose to spite their face. I never thought you'd be one of them.

Ronnie. I'll have to think about it, then, won't I?

Wilf. You won't tell me what you're going to do?

(Harry *comes from the kitchen into the hall and tries to hear the conversation*)

Ronnie. I've told you. I'm going to think about it.

Wilf. Harry won't be coming back to Bronhill for a few days so if you or anybody else wants him you can contact him through me. I'd be grateful if you didn't bother my mother for the time being. She'll be upset enough when she gets to know.

Ronnie (*rising and moving R*) It's a bit late for the sentimental approach, isn't it? Harry should have thought about all that before he attacked June.

Wilf. Y'know, Ronnie, you think too much in terms of black and white. It might be all right in politics but it won't do with people. Are you sure you know all there is to know about this business?

Ronnie. I know what June told me and what I saw for myself. That's good enough for me.

Wilf. You won't say here and now that you're going to drop the whole thing?

Ronnie. I've told you. I'll think it over. And your precious brother can sweat it out, wherever he is.

Wilf. You'd better have my number at the works. (*He takes out the photograph of June, writes a number on the back, then hands it to Ronnie*)

(Ronnie *glances at the number then casually turns the photograph over*)

Ronnie. Where did you get this?

Wilf. Does it matter?

Ronnie (*shouting*) I'm asking you where you got it.

Wilf. Harry picked it up in Sheffield some time ago. (*He plucks the photograph out of Ronnie's fingers, and puts it in his pocket*) I'll keep it in a safe place, don't worry.

Ronnie. You bastard! You low, cunning bastard!

WILF. I didn't want to bring it out, Ronnie, but you made me. You can see it was taken a long time ago, before she knew you, and nobody knows about it but Harry and me. You can't crucify a girl because she once posed for a pin-up picture. It doesn't have to mean anything; except that this business with Harry isn't as black and white as you thought.

RONNIE (*savagely*) I thought! D'you think I don't know? D'you think I could get June into court to say Harry tried to rape her? All that time when I thought we were friends he had that photo and he was thinking she was fair game. What did he need the photo for? Couldn't he tell without it? The bloke in Calderford hadn't any photo but he got the message. And *he* had her. It wasn't a bit of slap and tickle on the sofa with him. (*He sits on the desk chair*) He got the bloody jackpot on the back seat of his car.

(WILF *looks at Ronnie with compassion*)

WILF. Why did you come here tonight, Ronnie?

RONNIE. Because I don't know where she is. She's walked out.

WILF. You thought she might be with Harry?

RONNIE. I soon knew she wasn't from the way you were talking.

WILF. She'll come back. She's probably only trying to scare you.

RONNIE. Do I want her back, though? That's the point.

WILF. I'm sorry.

RONNIE. Yeh; you and everybody else. (*He rises. After a pause*) So you can tell him he's won.

WILF. Does anybody win in cases like this, Ronnie? Everybody ends up a bit sadder and wiser, that's all.

RONNIE (*moving to the door*) Don't spout your tuppence-ha'penny philosophy at me. Save it for your books. (*He goes into the hall*)

(HARRY, *surprised, steps quickly back. It is only as* RONNIE *is opening the front door that he sees* HARRY. *For a second they are arrested there, looking at each other without speaking.*

RONNIE *exits by the front door.* WILF *takes a box of matches from the mantelpiece, the photograph from his pocket and sets light to it.* HARRY *goes into* WILF's *room, and watches* WILF *as he drops the remains of the photograph into the ashtray.* WILF *turns and looks at Harry. When he speaks it is in no spirit of triumph, rather in a mood of disillusionment and disgust*)

WILF. That's that, then. C'mon, let's go and get that pint.

(HARRY *goes into the hall.* WILF *follows Harry into the hall, switching off the light as he goes.*

HARRY *and* WILF *exit by the front door. The* LIGHTS *dim to* BLACK-OUT *to indicate a passage of time. A church clock chimes in the distance. The* LIGHT *comes up in the hall.*

HARRY *and* WILF *enter by the front door. They have both drunk a fair amount but it is* WILF *who shows it, being a less practised drinker than Harry.* WILF *goes into his room and bumps into the armchair* C. HARRY *follows Wilf into the room.* WILF *slides to the floor*)

HARRY. Where's that flamin' light switch. (*He finds the switch and switches on the lights*) Ah!

(WILF *picks himself up from the floor*)

WILF. Who's been shifting the furniture about?

(HARRY *takes two pint bottles of beer from his pockets and puts them on the table*)

HARRY (*crossing to the fireplace*) Tell you what—we've forgotten the bloody fish 'n chips.
WILF. Too late. I'm past it.
HARRY. You're telling me, mate. I've never seen you sup like that before. I didn't think you could take so much.
WILF. I can't. I'm drunk. (*He removes his jacket and throws it towards the bed*) Let's have a bottle open, then.
HARRY. I thought you'd had enough.
WILF (*flopping into the armchair* C) I never said that. I said I was drunk. Which I am.

(HARRY *crosses to the table, opens one of the bottles of beer, pours some beer into the whisky glasses and hands one to Wilf*)

HARRY. I hope Ronnie hasn't got foot and mouth disease.
WILF (*raising his glass*) Here's to women. To Marguerite and her friend in the big white Jaguar.

(*They drink*)

And here's to Poppy and her long-lost husband whose half of the bed I've kept warm.

(HARRY *chokes on his drink*)

HARRY. You are a bloody dark horse, aren't you? I'd an idea you were up to summat there.
WILF. But not any longer. I'm now the cast-off lover, spurned for the sake of a spouse who done her wrong.
HARRY. She's not a widow at all, then?
WILF. No, last night she revealed all.
HARRY. And where the hell's her husband been all this time?
WILF. In and out of the nick as far as I can gather. And now he's coming home to make it up.
HARRY. Which means you'll be looking for new digs, I reckon.
WILF. Oh, no. Oh, no. I won't be pushed out like that. Mebbe he'll stay for a fortnight and get the wanderlust again.
HARRY (*crossing and sitting in the armchair* L) I could see me getting the wanderlust with Poppy to keep me warm at night.
WILF. Ah, but you're an upright gent, if a trifle lecherous; and Swallow is a cad; a bounder of the first water.
HARRY. You're a crafty snake, Wilf. There's more to you than meets the eye.

WILF. As I said before, my boy, there is to most people. Take our friend, Mrs Ronnie Betley.

HARRY. Aye, it's funny to think I could have had a real red-hot affair with her if only things had turned out a bit different.

WILF. Now don't start weaving fantasies on those lines again. There's been enough trouble caused there. Take my advice you'll clear out of Bronhill as soon as possible.

HARRY. You mean leave home an' live in digs?

WILF. Why not? You're a big lad now, Harry.

HARRY. It'd be a change, I suppose. It's worked wonders for you.

(WILF *reacts with an ironic snort*)

But I like living at home. It's cheaper and you get looked after better.

WILF. All I'm saying is that Ronnie won't forget all this and you're too big a target where you are.

(SYLVIA *enters by the front door, and hearing voices, lingers in the hall*)

HARRY. Mebbe you're right. I'll have to think about it.

(SYLVIA *has an idea and takes a cigarette from her handbag*)

WILF. Aye, you do that. (*He rises, moves to the bed and slumps down on his back with his legs over the edge*)

(SYLVIA *knocks on the door of Wilf's room.* HARRY *rises, crosses to the door and opens it*)

SYLVIA (*indicating the cigarette*) Oh, I'm sorry to bother you, but I saw the light. I wonder if you can spare me a match.

HARRY (*moving into the hall*) Oh, yes, aye. (*He takes out a box of matches, strikes one and holds it to Sylvia's cigarette*)

SYLVIA. Thanks ever so much. Can you spare me another for morning?

HARRY (*handing the box to her*) Here, have the box.

SYLVIA. Ooh, thanks. Y'know you are like that chap at the *Green Dragon*.

HARRY. I thought you said the *White Bull*.

SYLVIA. Did I? I must've got mixed up. Are you going to be here long?

HARRY (*suggestively*) That all depends on how much I like it.

SYLVIA. Well, happen I'll see you again before you go. (*She goes up the stairs but stops halfway and looks back at Harry*) Thanks again for the matches.

HARRY. That's all right, love. I'll be happy to light you up any time.

(SYLVIA *gives a little exclamatory giggle and exits up the stairs.* HARRY *watches her till she disappears, then goes to the foot of the stairs as though to follow her. At that moment* WILF *calls out without moving*)

WILF (*calling*) Harry!

(HARRY *turns back with a rueful shake of his head, goes into the room, pours himself more beer, then holds the bottle up to the light to see the level*)

HARRY. Do you want this last drop of ale, or have you had enough?

HARRY *goes to the recumbent* WILF *and sees that he is asleep. He stands looking meditatively at him, drinking at the same time, then he shakes his head affectionately, puts his glass on the table and bends down to unfasten Wilf's shoes as—*

the CURTAIN *falls*

SCENE 2

SCENE—*The same. An autumn night, ten weeks later.*

When the CURTAIN *rises, the scene is in darkness except for the hall light. Occasional noises of wind are heard throughout the scene.* WILF *enters by the front door, wearing a raincoat and muffler. He goes into his room, switches on the light, crosses to the gas fire, lights it and warms his hands. He straightens up, removes his coat and muffler and throws them across the bed. He runs a comb through his tousled hair, then takes a letter from his pocket. The envelope is open and from the way* WILF *glances at the letter it is obvious he has read it before.* MARGUERITE *enters by the front door. Her hair is windswept. She pauses at the foot of the stairs, looks up towards the landing and then at Wilf's door. She goes to the door, taps on it, opens it and looks in.*

MARGUERITE. Can I come in?

WILF. Yes, sure. Come in.

(MARGUERITE *enters and closes the door behind her. During the first part of this scene, until the quarrel,* WILF *is withdrawn and rather offhand with Marguerite. His mood is one of disillusionment and dejection over the letter and the events of the evening, and to this is added what he now recognizes as jealousy of Stephen Hollis whom Marguerite is still seeing*)

MARGUERITE. What a dreadful night. I can't wait for spring. (*During the early part of the conversation she makes efforts to tidy her hair*)

WILF. It is a bit wild.

MARGUERITE (*moving* c) I'm sorry to barge in on you but I want to let Swallow get out of the way before I go upstairs. I thought I heard his voice on the landing.

WILF. What's wrong, then? He doesn't come slobbering at you every time he sees you, does he?

MARGUERITE. Oh, I know you think I'm silly, but I just can't bear him.

WILF. He's not the most likeable character I've ever met. Take your coat off and come to the fire.

MARGUERITE. Well, just for a minute. (*She removes her coat and puts it on the armchair* C) He's just lost his latest job. Has Poppy told you? (*She moves to the fireplace*)

WILF. Yes. She says he's give it up because the dyes give him dermatitis. I think it's the thought of work that brings him out in a rash.

MARGUERITE (*kneeling at the fire and warming her hands*) It makes me squirm to see the way Poppy tries to justify what he does; especially when everybody can see how much they quarrel.

WILF. Yes, the second honeymoon's over there. And it hasn't taken long, either.

MARGUERITE. He frightens me. He seems to be always creeping about, on the prowl. I can't come in without meeting him, and a couple of days ago I got up in the middle of the night to go to the bathroom and when I opened my door he was there, standing on the landing with his back to me.

WILF. Did he say anything?

MARGUERITE. I didn't give him a chance. I shut the door again quickly, and when I looked out again in a few minutes he was gone.

WILF. He's no good, but he won't hurt you.

MARGUERITE. It's Poppy, though.

WILF. I know. She's looked very strained recently. Pale. I warned her what might happen when she first said he was coming. Anyway, it's their business, not ours. Have you been working over till this time?

MARGUERITE (*rising and moving* C) I worked till nine, then I went for a cup of coffee.

WILF. They're driving you a bit hard, aren't they, keeping you till nine, three nights a week?

MARGUERITE. Oh, I don't mind. (*She sits in the armchair* C) The money's always useful, and it's only for a short time, anyway.

WILF. You seem to have decided to stick around here for a while.

MARGUERITE. I suppose I have. When I first came back I told myself I'd make no plans; just live each day as it came. I suppose I'm still doing that.

WILF. Isn't there a problem you'll have to face some time?

MARGUERITE. You mean my father? I don't even know if he's still here. (*She changes the subject*) Wasn't it tonight you were going to that meeting about the Writers' Club?

WILF. Yes, I've been.

MARGUERITE. Are they going to form one?

WILF. Oh, I expect they'll form one. (*Moodily*) But I shan't be in it.

MARGUERITE. Was it as bad as that?

WILF (*sitting in the armchair* L) Just put me down as naïve. (*He takes his slippers from the hearth and changes his shoes*) I expected too much, that's all. They're just scribblers. A guinea for a letter here, a chatty little article on window-boxes there. "The one day I shall always remember." You know. There isn't a real writer among them. Not one.

Marguerite. I'll bet they were mostly women, too.

Wilf. How did you guess? Housewives young and old, dashing off hospital stories among the washing-up and the nappies. Oh, I know there are plenty of good women writers and some of them have to cope with a family as well as their work. But that lot simply don't know what real writing is.

Marguerite. But surely, talking to people with similar interests and problems can be stimulating.

Wilf. That lot couldn't stimulate me to write a laundry list.

Marguerite. I think you're being rather intolerant and arrogant about it.

Wilf (*rising and moving up* c) Perhaps I am. It's like I always say: it's failure that breeds arrogance. And you don't get much chance of forgetting it, stuck in a dump like this.

Marguerite. You chose the dump. Why didn't you get out when Swallow came back?

(*Now that* Wilf *is challenged he acts unreasonably*)

Wilf. Why should I have? What's that got to do with it?

Marguerite. I don't want to pry.

Wilf. Then don't.

Marguerite (*obviously hurt*) I'm sorry. I didn't mean . . .

Wilf. Look, I don't ask you questions. Why do you want to rake things up? I don't ask you about your life. I don't ask you what you get up to with young Hollis. I don't want to talk about it.

Marguerite. It sounds as though you think about it.

Wilf. I don't need to. I know that sort. I can guess every move in the game. A slap-up meal in some shiny roadhouse, a few stiff drinks and getting dressed a few hours later in a lay-by.

Marguerite (*near to tears*) My God, you do think about it, don't you? Well, you're not as smart as you think. Stephen is a kind person.

Wilf. A gentleman! (*He moves and slumps on to the bed*)

Marguerite. Yes, if you like. All right, he's got money. There's nothing wrong with that. It might interest you to know that he's asked me to marry him.

Wilf. Well done, well done! I take it all back. When's the big day to be?

Marguerite. I suppose it couldn't occur to you that I might have said "No"?

Wilf. Why should you say "No"? He's got everything a girl could want, hasn't he?

Marguerite. How do you know what a girl wants? What I want? What do you know about me, anyway?

Wilf. I'm not blind.

Marguerite (*rising*) Yes, you are blind. You judge everybody

D

by your own splendid principles and they all fall short. You walk about in your own self-pitying little world and you don't see a thing about anybody else. (*She turns away so that Wilf will not see how near she is to crying*)

WILF (*realizing he has gone too far*) I'm sorry. I'm sorry. (*He rises and moves to her*) You're right about the self-pity. I've been wallowing in it all day. This came this morning. (*He takes out the letter and hands it to Marguerite then moves R*)

MARGUERITE. What is it?

WILF. They've turned the novel down. Read it for yourself.

(MARGUERITE *reads the letter and now the tears come*)

(*He recites the contents of the letter from memory*) "Dear Sir, We have read the manuscript of your novel with considerable interest and feel that this is a well-written carefully worked-out story which shows a good deal of ability, particularly in the dialogue passages. After careful consideration, however, we feel that it would appeal to only a limited audience and we are, therefore, unable to make you an offer of publication. Et cetera, et cetera, et cetera." You see, I can recite it from memory. (*He pauses*) So that's that. You spend a couple of years putting everything you know into a book till you just know it's good. And then that. Dismissed in half a dozen lines. And I could hear them going through my head while I was with those people. Who am I to be arrogant—(*he pauses*) about anything? (*He notices that Marguerite is crying*) Marguerite. I said I'm sorry, and I am. (*He moves to her and takes her by the shoulders from behind*) Marguerite, don't cry. Ah, love, don't cry. (*He turns her round and looks at her*)

MARGUERITE (*gently trying to extricate herself*) I'd better be going.

WILF. No, don't go. Oh, God, I'm so jealous I can't see straight.

MARGUERITE (*freeing herself*) No, you can't see what should be obvious. (*She crosses to the fireplace*)

WILF. You mean . . . ?

MARGUERITE (*turning to him*) I mean, I should have thought it was plain enough for anybody to see. Poppy knew.

WILF (*crossing to Marguerite and placing his hands on her shoulders*) Marguerite, about Poppy and me. It was good while it lasted, but it was nothing like this.

MARGUERITE. Please, Wilf, don't say anything you'll regret.

WILF. No. Stone-cold sober, remember? I am jealous of Hollis and I'm miserable about the novel, but I know what I'm saying. (*He holds her more closely*)

(*They kiss. Eventually* MARGUERITE *pulls away*)

MARGUERITE. I hate to be unromantic, but the fire's burning my legs.

(WILF *laughs, takes her hand and sits in the armchair* L. MARGUERITE *curls up on the floor by his legs*)

Just listen to that wind.

Wilf. Mmm.

Marguerite. There'll be slates off in the morning.

Wilf. I shouldn't wonder.

(Marguerite *looks at the ceiling as though she has heard something*)

Marguerite. Wasn't that a bump from upstairs?

Wilf. Probably Poppy pushing Swallow out of bed.

Marguerite. I can't joke about that man.

Wilf. And I can't concern myself with anyone's unhappiness tonight. When *did* friend Hollis fade out of the picture?

Marguerite. He was never really in it; not in that way. I suppose I used him as a kind of antidote. You see, when I first came here I thought it would be a long time before I looked twice at a man.

Wilf. Ah, I've wondered about that.

Marguerite. It's a commonplace story, I suppose. He was an American working over here. I never asked for anything. I knew he'd have to go home eventually, but I left the future to work itself out. What I didn't know was that he had a wife and family in the States. It had all been decided from the beginning. There wasn't any future for us. There never had been. When I found out I simply ran for cover. I couldn't bear to face him again. This was the only place I could think of apart from Amhurst, and I didn't want to go back there.

Wilf. You're sure you're really over it now?

Marguerite. Oh, yes, quite sure.

Wilf. I'm glad. I'm glad because as far as you're concerned I don't want any short-lived affair.

Marguerite. Wilf, please—I'm not asking you for anything, either.

Wilf. But I'm asking you. I want everything you can give me. But slowly. I don't want to spoil a single minute of it. I want all of you, but I want the promise first. And I just can't believe it. I can't believe it, even now.

Marguerite. Oh, it's true, darling, it's true.

Wilf. Will you come home with me this weekend? I'd like you to.

Marguerite. Oh, dear! To face the family.

Wilf. Well, there's only mum and dad.

Marguerite. What about your mysterious brother—Harry?

Wilf. Eh? You mean you never met him when he came here?

Marguerite. No, you kept him to yourself, but he seems to have made an impression on Sylvia.

Wilf. He would. Anyway, he's working away now.

Marguerite. Your mother, is she fierce?

Wilf (*laughing*) She can be. But she'll love you. Just don't go all cool and lofty on her, that's all. You have a very effective daughter-of-the-earl air that you switch on when you think people are getting at you.

MARGUERITE (*laughing*) I know. I watch myself doing it. (*She quotes herself*) "I think we can take it, Mr Cotton, that my views on the colour question are as enlightened as yours." And then I went upstairs and had a little weep because I thought I was getting off on the wrong foot here as well. It's a defence I developed when I went to Amhurst. I didn't fit in at school there at first. They used to mimic my accent and for a while I was too proud to try to copy theirs. But time took care of that. After eighteen months you couldn't tell me from the rest of them. I only switched back to Yorkshire to make people laugh.

WILF. Do it now.

MARGUERITE. Ah luv thee, lad.

(WILF *is suddenly deeply moved. He takes Marguerite's hand and presses it to his cheek*)

WILF. Marguerite. What about your father and what happened when you were a kid?

MARGUERITE. Oh, that . . .

WILF. Come on, love, get rid of it. Hasn't it haunted you for long enough?

MARGUERITE (*after a pause*) I had a brother and sister, younger than me. Peter and Angela. There was a woman called Laura who came to live with us after my mother died. She and my father used to go out a lot. One night when I was looking after the children there was a fire. I was across the road with a friend. Peter was always playing with matches. They said at the inquest that he'd crept downstairs and tried to light the paraffin stove, and locked the door to stop me catching him. They were both suffocated. (*She pauses*) I went to have a look just after I came back. The row was due for demolition and we were the last family living there. I thought all the houses would be down now but they were still there, with their roofs off, just as they were all that long time ago. My father took it out on me. He beat me and he went to prison for it. I went to live with my uncle and aunt and I never saw him again.

WILF. I don't blame you for not looking for him.

MARGUERITE. No—but I can't leave it like that. I've always intended to try to find him, but I knew I'd have to wait for the right time, I had to wait until I was strong enough to accept whatever I found. So that even if it was the worst it couldn't hurt me.

WILF. You think perhaps you could do it now?

MARGUERITE (*looking at him*) Yes, I think I could now.

WILF. Oh, my love, my little love. (*He slips to the floor beside Marguerite and kisses her*)

MARGUERITE. What time is it?

WILF. Time all respectable people were in bed.

MARGUERITE. Will you think about me when you're falling asleep?

WILF. I don't know if I will sleep; I've got so much to think about.

MARGUERITE. I'll think about you. And in the morning, in that tiny instant between sleeping and waking, I'll open my eyes and think that nothing's different, that everything's like it was this morning. And then I'll remember. It'll all come rushing in.

(*They rise and suddenly* MARGUERITE *is clinging to Wilf, both arms round his chest*)

WILF. What is it, Marguerite? What's wrong, love?
MARGUERITE. Nothing. I'm just being silly.
WILF. You know, I always told Poppy I didn't want to be saddled with a woman; but I wasn't counting on anything like this happening. Now I know that when it does happen everything else seems to fit into place. I feel like a man who's discovered the secret of the universe.
MARGUERITE. You know, for a realistic novelist, you've got a very romantic mind.
WILF. But you won't tell anybody, will you?

(MARGUERITE *laughs, gives Wilf a peck on the mouth, then begins to gather her things*)

MARGUERITE. No, I promise. You will send the novel away again, won't you?
WILF. As soon as it comes back.
MARGUERITE. It is good, you know.
WILF. I'll take your word for it. (*He crosses to the door and opens it*)
MARGUERITE (*following Wilf to the door*) Good night, then.
WILF. Good night, love. I'll see you in the morning.

(MARGUERITE *suddenly grasps Wilf's arm*)

MARGUERITE. Did you hear that?
WILF. What?
MARGUERITE. Something upstairs.

(*They listen*)

WILF. It's only the wind.
MARGUERITE. It sounded like something else. I can't hear it now.
WILF. That bloke really has got you down, hasn't he? Do you want me to come up with you?
MARGUERITE. No, it'll be all right. I must go.

(*They cling together briefly then go into the hall.* MARGUERITE *goes up the stairs, pauses a moment and waves to* WILF *who waves back before going into his room and closing the door.*
MARGUERITE *exits up the stairs.* WILF *crosses to the fireplace, looking very pleased with himself, then turns back his bed and sets out his pyjamas.* MARGUERITE, *off, is heard to scream.* WILF, *startled, rushes into the hall.*
MARGUERITE *enters at the top of the stairs*)

D*

WILF. Marguerite, what's wrong?
MARGUERITE. It's Poppy. Wilf, she's lying on the floor and there's blood all over her face.

WILF *starts up the stairs as—*

the CURTAIN *falls*

SCENE 3

SCENE—*The same. Late afternoon, two weeks later.*

When the CURTAIN *rises,* WILF *enters by the front door. He is wearing his raincoat and muffler. He stands in the open doorway for a moment, looking back, before closing the door and coming into the hall.* SYLVIA *enters at the top of the stairs and talks to Wilf over the banister rail.*

SYLVIA. You're back, then. I thought I heard the door. Where's Poppy?
WILF. Talking to somebody outside. Sensation-seekers. I wish they'd leave her alone.
SYLVIA. Is she all right?
WILF. A bit tired. And thanking her lucky stars it wasn't worse.
SYLVIA. He must be a bloody madman.
WILF. Well, they've got him safely under lock and key and I reckon he'll have a long time to think things over this time.
SYLVIA. He'd never come out again if I had owt to do with it. You could see straight away 'at he was a wrong 'un. It was all he came back for, y'know—because he thought Poppy had some money tucked away. He could have killed her—you know that? I told her she wanted her head seeing to.
WILF (*flatly*) She got it seen to. (*He removes his coat and muffler and hangs them in the hall*)
SYLVIA. What? Well, that's not a very funny thing to say, is it?
WILF. Look, Sylvia, she'll be in in a minute and she wants to be quiet. Would you mind making yourself scarce and not upsetting her.
SYLVIA (*a little huffily*) Oh, all right. I'm going out in a minute but if there's anything she wants before then you can give me a shout.
WILF. Yes, all right.

(SYLVIA *exits up the stairs.* WILF *goes into his room.*
POPPY *enters by the front door and goes into Wilf's room. She is looking about her*)

Ah, there you are, Poppy. I was just thinking about coming to rescue you.

Poppy. Funny how things seem just that little bit different—you know, out of focus, like—even when you've only been away a fortnight.

Wilf. Well, you're home again now, love, safe and sound, and that's all that matters.

(Poppy *sighs and sits in the armchair* c)

Poppy (*loosening her coat*) Aye, it could have been worse, I suppose. I shall have to think of it that way. On the face of it, I suppose I was daft for taking Alf back. Still, I gave him a chance, I did the best I could. If I'd turned him away I'd never have stopped wondering if I'd done the right thing.

Wilf (*moving to* L *of Poppy*) What are you going to do now, Poppy? Got any plans?

Poppy. Yes, I have. I did a lot of thinking while I was lying in hospital. I've decided to move away from here. I think I'm going to look for a boarding-house at the seaside.

Wilf. You're sure it won't be too much for you?

Poppy. Oh, I shall soon be as good as new again. I'm tough, you know. (*She removes her scarf*)

Wilf. Yes, I can just see you. Like on the postcards. A great tough, aggressive landlady bashing all the kids with their buckets.

Poppy. Get on with you. What about you, though? Have you heard anything about that book?

Wilf. Well, the first publisher I sent it to turned it down; but I've had a letter from an agent saying he thinks he can do something with it.

Poppy. Well, that's grand. (*She rises and puts her scarf on the table*)

Wilf. Yes, it is.

Poppy. You don't seem to be doing much cheering.

Wilf. Oh, it's great, Poppy, but somehow I can't feel delirious about it. The trouble is, you know, that you can't have what you want when you want it. You get it tomorrow and tomorrow's a different day. Life's moved on and you've moved with it. I'm a different person from the one who finished that book and sent it out. I hope I'm a, well, a bigger person. (*He pauses*) Poppy, Marguerite and I are going to get married.

Poppy. Is that true? Oh, Wilf, I am glad. (*She embraces Wilf briefly*) Well, don't look so timid. I *am* glad. I always thought you two ought to hit it off. When did all this happen?

Wilf. It was the night Swallow attacked you. If we hadn't been so wrapped up in each other we might have heard what was going on.

Poppy. She knows about us, does she?

Wilf. I didn't have to tell her; she'd already guessed.

Poppy. She knows what's what, does that lass. She's had her own troubles.

Wilf. Yes. How much do you know?

Poppy (*sitting in the armchair* c) Nearly all of it, I suppose. Marguerite had a heart-to-heart talk with me some time ago. It was after she'd been out with that Hollis chap one time. I knew then it was you she wanted, though I don't think she knew it herself.

WILF. Oh, come on now, Poppy. Your imagination. You know you were always dropping hints about the two of us.

POPPY. Well, why didn't she go for Hollis, then? He was a much better catch than you.

WILF. True enough.

POPPY. But she never really wanted him. She guessed early on that she could get him if she tried and she was scared she might take him in spite of herself, because she was lonely and looking for somebody in her life.

WILF. You're a good soul, Poppy, and I'll never forget what we had together. I hope you'll be happy when you get settled down.

POPPY. Don't you worry about me. You just take care of that lass. Make *her* happy. She deserves it. You do love her, don't you?

WILF (*quietly*) Yes, I do. (*He takes Poppy's hand*) You know I'll always be fond of you, love.

POPPY. I should hope so. But don't you mix that up with what you feel for Marguerite. You know the difference.

WILF. Yes. But look at me standing here gabbing. You must want a cup of tea.

POPPY. I'll make one in a minute.

WILF. No, you won't. You'll stay right there. I'll go and do it. I won't be long, and Marguerite should be home any time.

(WILF *goes into the hall, crosses the kitchen and exits to the scullery.* POPPY *rises and wanders about the room. She runs her finger along the mantelpiece and frowns with distaste at the dust. She crosses to the table and sits at it, putting both hands on Wilf's typewriter with an action that is full of suppressed tenderness.*

SYLVIA *enters down the stairs and seeing Wilf's door open, looks into the room. Seeing Poppy alone she enters*)

SYLVIA. Hello, Poppy. It's nice to see you back.

POPPY. Hello, Sylvia. How's life treating you?

SYLVIA. Oh, so so. Can't grumble. No more than usual, anyway. (*She moves* C) Where's Wilf?

POPPY. He's making a cup of tea.

SYLVIA. Did you have a taxi home?

POPPY. Yes, Wilf saw to that.

SYLVIA (*hesitantly*) And you're all right, are you?

POPPY. I'm coming round. It takes more than a knock on the head to put me out of action.

SYLVIA (*hesitantly*) I didn't mean that exactly.

POPPY. What did you mean, then?

SYLVIA. You know what I'm talking about, Poppy. You can't hide a thing like that for long, y'know. You can read it in a woman's face.

(POPPY *is startled and reacts almost ferociously*)

POPPY. You haven't said anything to them, have you?

SYLVIA. It's not my place to tell 'em. (*She sits on the right arm of the armchair* L) But Wilf'll have to know, won't he?

POPPY. What's it got to do with him? I'll tell 'em in my own good time. Not that it's any of their business, if it comes to that. You know they're getting married, do you?

SYLVIA. I didn't know. But a blind man could see there was summat between them. They walk about as if there was nobody else in the world but them. It'd be a pity to spoil it.

POPPY. Nobody's going to spoil it, Sylvia. They're right for each other.

SYLVIA. Is that all that matters, then?

POPPY. Well, isn't it?

SYLVIA. There'd be a hell of a sight more than that mattered if it was me.

POPPY (*rising*) Look here. (*She crosses to Sylvia*) There was something between Wilf and me at one time. I'm not denying that and Marguerite knows about it. But there never was any future in it and it finished when Alf came back. I've been a married woman again for near three months, Sylvia, *living with my husband*. I don't know what funny ideas you've got in your head, but if you say anything out of turn, I'll strangle you with my two hands.

SYLVIA. Oh, I can carry corn. But you can't stop me from thinking you're a fool. You were a fool for taking your husband back and you're a worse fool for doing what you're going to do now.

POPPY. No, Sylvia, you're the fool. You can't measure everything by a few bright lights, a couple of free drinks, and a giggle in the back of a car.

SYLVIA. So he's going to get away with it.

POPPY. I don't know what you're talking about.

SYLVIA. You can tell that to the vicar.

POPPY. Look, Sylvia, what's the matter? What's it got to do with you, anyway?

SYLVIA. It's got nothing to do with me. I know that. But he's so flamin' superior when he talks. Thinks he's so clever. Bloody men, they always get the best of it. And we're so stupid you'd think we enjoyed being walked on.

(MARGUERITE *enters by the front door*)

(*She hears Marguerite and rises*) That'll be her ladyship, I suppose. Well, I've said my piece so I'd better be off. (*She crosses and goes into the hall*)

MARGUERITE. Hello, Sylvia. Just going out?

SYLVIA (*dryly*) Aye, I've got a date with some bright lights. Poppy's in there.

(SYLVIA *exits by the front door.* MARGUERITE *goes into Wilf's room*)

MARGUERITE. Hello, Poppy. (*She crosses and briefly embraces Poppy*) Those rush hour buses get worse. I wanted to be back to welcome you with a cup of tea. Are you all right?

POPPY. Yes, I'm all right. Wilf's seeing to the tea. (*She sits in the armchair* c)

(MARGUERITE *removes her coat and lays it on the bed.*
WILF *enters from the scullery, crosses and goes into the hall. He carries a tray of tea for three. He taps on his door with his foot.* MARGUERITE *moves to the door and opens it*)

WILF (*coming into the room*) You see, I'm quite domesticated, for all my faults. (*He kisses Marguerite on the cheek*)

(MARGUERITE *throws a quick glance at* POPPY *who has apparently not noticed*)

(*He puts the tray on the table*) There. We'll just give that a minute to mash.

POPPY. I've got a bone to pick with you, young woman.

MARGUERITE. Oh?

POPPY. Aye, you've been keeping secrets from me.

(MARGUERITE *looks at* WILF, *who nods and smiles*)

MARGUERITE. Wilf's told you, then?

POPPY. He has, and I'm pleased, love.

MARGUERITE. We didn't want to keep it from you, Poppy, but it seemed wrong for us to be happy when you had so much trouble.

POPPY. I wish you all the happiness in the world, and if you don't let me help you with the wedding I'll never forgive you. When is it going to be, then? Come on, tell me all about it.

WILF. Soon, Poppy.

MARGUERITE. We haven't made any definite plans yet. (*She sits on the right end of the bed*)

WILF. Marguerite wants to try and find her father. If we can and it's all right, she hopes he'll give her away.

POPPY. How can you find him? Will you advertise or something?

WILF. We'd thought of searching the Electoral Roll. That way we'd find him if he's still here.

POPPY. And suppose he isn't here any more?

WILF. Then we'll just have to forget about him for the time being.

MARGUERITE. There's something we haven't thought of. My name was in the paper the other week, along with yours and Wilf's. And it'll be in again when the trial comes on.

WILF. Yes, of course. I hadn't thought of that. He might come looking for *you*.

MARGUERITE. Yes.

POPPY (*rising briskly*) Well, I advise you to face that when it comes and not before. I vote we have a cup of tea.

MARGUERITE. Oh, stay where you are, Poppy. I'll do it. (*She rises*)

POPPY (*pushing Marguerite aside*) No, you won't. (*She moves to the table, sits at it and pours the tea*) I'm still mistress in my own house, and quite capable of pouring a cup of tea. One sugar for Wilf, none for you, Marguerite, and none for me. That's right, isn't it? Why didn't you use that brown pot, Wilf? It makes much better tea.

WILF (*pulling a face*) Er—brace yourself, Poppy. I had an accident with it last week.

POPPY. Good to tell I've been away. (*She rises and hands cups of tea to Wilf and Marguerite*) There we are, then. Now, you can brace yourselves because I've got a piece of news for you. I'm going to have a baby.

MARGUERITE. Poppy! A baby!

POPPY. That's what I said. After all these years. Will you look at his face.

WILF. You mean . . . ?

POPPY. Now what do you think I mean? Use your common sense, lad.

WILF. But do you want it?

POPPY. Of course I want it. (*She sits in the armchair* C) If you knew the hours I'd pined for a bairn. Aye, and now I'm having one. Better late than never. It won't have a father's love but by God it'll get enough mother-love to make up for it. (*She is suddenly crying*)

(MARGUERITE *crosses, puts her cup on the table* R, *then turns and embraces Poppy*)

MARGUERITE. Oh, Poppy, do take care of yourself, won't you?

POPPY. Of course I shall. You don't need to worry about me.

MARGUERITE (*crossing and sitting on the right end of the bed*) Oh, isn't it wonderful, Wilf? I could hug myself.

WILF (*still rather bewildered*) Yes. (*He shakes it off*) Here we are, drinking tea with all this happening. We should be out somewhere celebrating.

POPPY. You two go, if you want to, but I've had enough excitement for one day.

WILF (*putting his cup on the table* R) Anyway, I've got something better than tea. (*He crosses to the cabinet down* L *and takes the remains of a bottle of whisky from the cupboard*) Look!

MARGUERITE. Whisky? Where did you get that?

WILF. A legacy from Harry. (*He takes three tumblers out of the cupboard, hands one each to Marguerite and Poppy and slops whisky into them*)

MARGUERITE. Oh, go steady.

(*They laugh.* WILF *pours some whisky into his own glass, puts the bottle on the table, then crosses and stands between Poppy and Marguerite*)

WILF. Now then. Here's to us.

POPPY (*dryly*) That's not much of a speech. Shortest I've ever heard from you.

MARGUERITE. Yes, come on. You've got a good excuse.

WILF (*posing*) A little folk poem, entitled *Grit*.

MARGUERITE (*laughing*) Come on, you can do better than that.

WILF (*seriously*) When you come right down to it, there isn't much to say. This is the end of something for all of us, and the beginning of something else.

MARGUERITE. I'm all for happy endings.

POPPY. And so am I, love.

WILF (*pretending to be shocked*) I've never written a happy ending in my life.

POPPY. Perhaps you wouldn't know one if you saw it.

WILF (*light-heartedly*) Well, if you know so much about it, Poppy, you give us a speech.

MARGUERITE. Yes, that's a good idea.

POPPY. Now don't you start on me.

WILF. No, come on, Poppy. Just a few words. You've got a good audience.

POPPY. I can't make speeches. When I'm happy I just cry.

WILF (*cheerfully*) Well, for God's sake don't cry now. We're celebrating. Aren't we? Well, aren't we?

(*There is a momentary hesitation on* POPPY's *part. Is the baby Wilf's? Sylvia certainly thinks so, but if* POPPY *does she is not going to let them suspect. She knows that she and Wilf could never have had a lasting relationship and she is happy about him and Marguerite as she is also about the child. When she lifts her glass it is in the realization that for a person of her age happiness can never be the unambiguous thing that it is to Wilf and Marguerite now*)

POPPY (*raising her glass*) Yes, you're right. Of course we are.

They drink as—

the CURTAIN *falls*

FURNITURE AND PROPERTY LIST

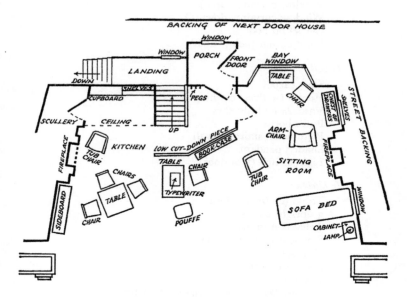

ACT I

SCENE 1

On stage: In Wilf's room:

Table (R) *On it:* portable typewriter, papers, typescript, folders, notebooks, typing paper, desk lamp

2 upright chairs

Wing armchair (L) *On it:* cushion

Armchair (C)

Pouffe

Low bookshelves (up R)
   On them: transistor radio, ornaments
   In them: books, magazines

Hooks (up R) *On them:* dressing-gown, clothing

Table (up C) *On it:* litter of books, magazines, etc.

Hooks (up L) *On them:* clothing

Chest of drawers (up L) *On it:* record-player, records

On wall over chest of drawers: bookshelves. *In them:* magazines, copy of *Etude*

Divan bed. *On it:* bedding and cover

Cabinet (down L) *On it:* table-lamp
Gas fire
On mantelpiece: clock, ashtray, matches, photographs, letters,
    ornaments
On wall over fireplace: pictures, 2 wall-brackets
Window curtains (up C)
Window curtains (down L)
Carpet on floor
Light switch (below door)

In hall:

Stair carpet
Hooks. *On them:* clothing
Vase. *In it:* bulrushes
Bull's horns
Pictures on staircase wall
Shaded pendant
Light switch (L of door)

In kitchen:

Table (C) *On it:* cloth
3 upright chairs
Television receiver
Sideboard. *On it:* china
Coal scuttle
Fire with oven
Fire-irons
On mantelpiece: clock, ornaments, ashtray
Over mantelpiece: picture
Armchair
Shelves (up C) *On them:* dry goods, china, mugs, etc.
Creel. *On it:* freshly ironed clothes
Carpet on floor
Shaded pendant
Light switch (up R)

Light fittings off
Window curtains open
Windows closed
All doors closed
Fire in Wilf's room, on

Off stage: Glass of milk (WILF)
Suitcase (MARGUERITE)
Shopping bag (POPPY)
Crash helmet (HARRY)

Personal: MARGUERITE: handbag. *In it:* cigarettes
HARRY: wallet with photograph
SYLVIA: handbag

SCENE 2

Strike: Glass
Crash helmet
Clothes from creel

Set: *On creel:* fresh clothes
On kitchen table: 2 ironed shirts
On living-room table: Marguerite's handbag
In typewriter: sheet of quarto paper
Wall-brackets on
Hall light on
Window curtains closed
Windows closed
All doors closed
Fire in Wilf's room, on

Personal: POPPY: handkerchief

SCENE 3

Set: *On kitchen table:* jug with cocoa, cup and saucer, basin of sugar, tea-
spoon
In kitchen cupboard: basin with dripping, cut loaf, 2 small plates, small
knife
Wilf's room in darkness
Window curtains closed
Windows closed
All doors closed
Fire off
Kitchen light on
Hall light on

Personal: MARGUERITE: handkerchief, scarf, handbag
SYLVIA: brooch on overcoat, handbag. *In it:* lipstick, compact

ACT II

SCENE I

Strike: Dripping, bread, 2 plates, knife, jug of cocoa, dirty cup, aspirin,
sugar

Set: *In kitchen:* ironing-board, iron
On mantelpiece: letter behind clock
On creel: clothes for ironing

Lower creel
Window curtains closed
Windows closed
All doors shut
Kitchen light on
Hall light on
Wall-brackets on
Desk lamp on
Fire off

Off stage: 2 bottles of beer, bottle opener, 2 glasses (WILF)

Personal: SYLVIA: handbag
MARGUERITE: handbag

SCENE 2

Strike: Beer bottles, glasses
Iron
Ironing-board
Ironed clothes
Letter

Set: *On bed:* 2 folded blankets
Window curtains closed
Windows closed
All doors shut
Kitchen light on
Hall light on
Fire on

Personal: HARRY: cigarettes, lighter, watch
WILF: watch

ACT III

SCENE 1

Strike: Blankets

Set: *On table in Wilf's room:* opened bottle of whisky, 2 tumblers
On armchair L: magazine
On bed: Harry's jacket
Tidy room generally
Window curtains open
Windows closed

All doors shut
Hall light on
Wall-brackets on
Fire on

Off stage: 2 bottles of beer (HARRY)

Personal: HARRY: watch, matches
WILF: photograph, ball-point pen
SYLVIA: handbag. *In it:* packet of cigarettes

SCENE 2

Strike: Beer bottles, dirty glasses
Magazine
Whisky bottle

Set: *Under bed cover:* Wilf's pyjamas
In hearth: Wilf's slippers
Window curtains closed
Windows closed
All doors closed
Hall light on
Other lights off
Fire off

Personal: WILF: raincoat, muffler, comb, letter
MARGUERITE: handbag. *In it:* handkerchief

SCENE 3

Strike: Wilf's shoes
Wilf's pyjamas

Set: *In bedside chest:* bottle of whisky, half full, 3 tumblers
Window curtains open
Windows closed
All doors closed
Light fittings off
Fire off

Off stage: Tray. *On it:* pot of tea, milk jug, sugar basin, 3 teaspoons, 3 cups,
3 saucers

Personal: POPPY: scarf, handbag
MARGUERITE: handbag
SYLVIA: handbag

LIGHTING PLOT

Property fittings required: 2 shaded pendants, 2 wall-brackets, desk lamp, table-lamp, fire

Interior. A composite set with kitchen R, hall C and living-room L. The same setting throughout

THE APPARENT SOURCES OF LIGHT are, in the kitchen, a pendant C; in the hall, in daytime, a window up R, and at night, a pendant C; in the living-room, in daytime, windows up C and down L, and at night, wall-brackets L, and table-lamps R and down L

THE MAIN ACTING AREAS are, in the kitchen, R; in the hall, C; and in the living-room, R, C and L

ACT I, SCENE 1. A midsummer afternoon

To open: Fittings off
General effect of dull daylight
Fire in living-room, on

No cues

ACT I, SCENE 2. Evening

To open: Fire in living-room, on
Wall-brackets, on
Hall light on
Other fittings out
Dark outside windows

No cues

ACT I, SCENE 3. Evening

To open: Fire out
Kitchen light on
Hall light on
Other fittings out
Dark outside windows

No cues

ACT II, SCENE 1. Evening

To open: Kitchen light on
Hall light on
Wall-brackets on
Desk lamp on
Fire out
Dark outside windows

Cue 1	WILF switches off desk lamp	(Page 25)
	Snap out desk lamp	
	Snap out covering lights	
Cue 2	WILF switches off wall-brackets	(Page 25)
	Snap out wall-brackets	
	Snap out covering lights	

ACT II, SCENE 2. Evening

To open: Hall light on
Kitchen light on
Fire on
Table-lamp on
Dark outside windows

Cue 3	POPPY switches off kitchen light	(Page 29)
	Snap out kitchen light	
	Snap out covering lights	
Cue 4	WILF switches on wall-brackets	(Page 30)
	Snap in wall-brackets	
	Snap in covering lights	

ACT III, SCENE 1. Evening

To open: Wall-brackets on
Hall light on
Fire on
Dark outside windows

Cue 5	WILF switches off wall-brackets	(Page 40)
	Snap out wall-brackets	
	Snap out covering lights	
Cue 6	WILF and HARRY exit	(Page 40)
	Dim all lights to BLACK-OUT *for a few moments to indicate*	
	a passage of time	
Cue 7	HARRY and WILF enter	(Page 40)
	Bring in hall light	
	Bring in covering light	
Cue 8	HARRY switches on wall-brackets	(Page 41)
	Snap in wall-brackets	
	Snap in covering lights	

ACT III, SCENE 2. Night

To open: Hall light on
Other lights out
Fire out
Dark outside windows

Cue 9	WILF switches on wall-brackets	(Page 43)
	Snap in wall-brackets	
	Snap in covering lights	

Cue 10   ·WILF lights fire   (Page 43)
           Bring in fire glow

ACT III, SCENE 3.   Late afternoon
To open: Effect of afternoon sunshine
           Fire off
           Fittings off
No cues

EFFECTS

ACT I

SCENE 1

Cue 1   WILF drinks   (Page 2)
         Door bell rings
Cue 2   POPPY: ". . . work to do."   (Page 8)
         Door bell rings

SCENE 2

No cues

SCENE 3

No cues

ACT II

SCENE 1

Cue 3   At rise of CURTAIN   (Page 24)
         Sound of a high-powered car arriving and stopping
Cue 4   MARGUERITE *exits*   (Page 25)
         Sound of the car starting up and driving away

SCENE 2

Cue 5   MARGUERITE *enters*   (Page 29)
         Sound of car starting up and departing

ACT III

SCENE 1

Cue 6   HARRY goes into the kitchen   (Page 37)
         Front-door bell rings
Cue 7   During BLACK-OUT   (Page 40)
         A church clock chimes

SCENE 2

Cue 8   After rise of CURTAIN   (Page 43)
         Occasional noises of wind throughout the scene

SCENE 3

No cues

Any character costumes or wigs needed in the performance of this play
can be hired from Charles H. Fox Ltd, 184 High Holborn, London W.C.1

MADE AND PRINTED IN GREAT BRITAIN BY
LATIMER TREND AND CO. LTD, PLYMOUTH
MADE IN ENGLAND

Lightning Source UK Ltd.
Milton Keynes UK
UKHW020955110422
401398UK00006B/428